BRAZILIAN JIU-JITSU

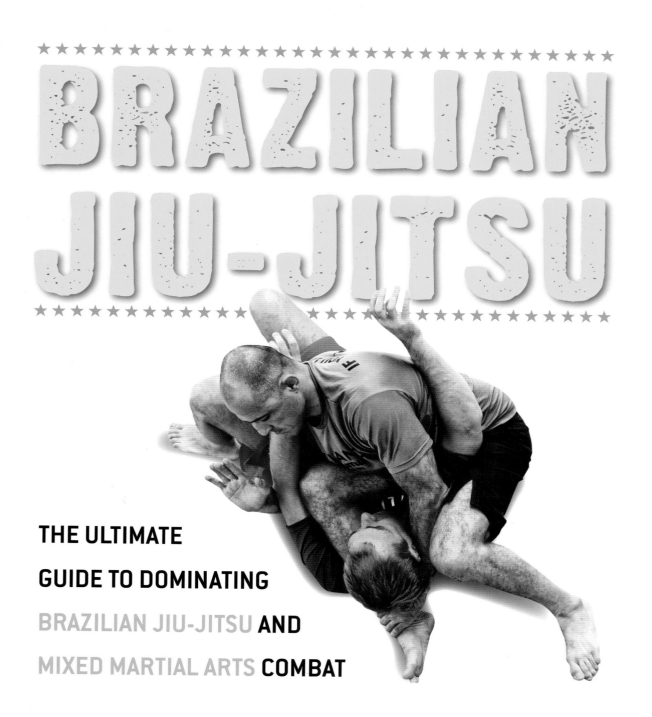

THE ULTIMATE
GUIDE TO DOMINATING
BRAZILIAN JIU-JITSU AND
MIXED MARTIAL ARTS COMBAT

TUTTLE Publishing

Tokyo | Rutland, Vermont | Singapore

T0354211

CONTENTS

"Books to Span the East and West"

Tuttle Publishing was founded in 1832 in the small New England town of Rutland, Vermont [USA]. Our core values remain as strong today as they were then—to publish best-in-class books which bring people together one page at a time. In 1948, we established a publishing outpost in Japan—and Tuttle is now a leader in publishing English-language books about the arts, languages and cultures of Asia. The world has become a much smaller place today and Asia's economic and cultural influence has grown. Yet the need for meaningful dialogue and information about this diverse region has never been greater. Over the past seven decades, Tuttle has published thousands of books on subjects ranging from martial arts and paper crafts to language learning and literature—and our talented authors, illustrators, designers and photographers have won many prestigious awards. We welcome you to explore the wealth of information available on Asia at **www.tuttlepublishing.com.**

Please note that the publisher and author(s) of this instructional book are NOT RESPONSIBLE in any manner whatsoever for any injury that may result from practicing the techniques and/or following the instructions given within. Martial arts training can be dangerous—both to you and to others—if not practiced safely. If you're in doubt as to how to proceed or whether your practice is safe, consult with a trained martial arts teacher before beginning. Since the physical activities described herein may be too strenuous in nature for some readers, it is also essential that a physician be consulted prior to training.

Published by Tuttle Publishing, an imprint of Periplus Editions (HK) Ltd.

www.tuttlepublishing.com

Copyright © 2012 Marian Bornakowski - Poznań, Poland
Photographs and graphic design: Marian Winiecki

All rights reserved. No part of this publication may be reproduced or utilized in any form or by any means, electronic or mechanical, including photocopying, recording, or by any information storage and retrieval system, without prior written permission from the publisher.

ISBN 978-0-8048-4275-4

Distributed by

North America, Latin America & Europe
Tuttle Publishing
364 Innovation Drive
North Clarendon
VT 05759-9436 U.S.A.
Tel: 1 (802) 773-8930
Fax: 1 (802) 773-6993
info@tuttlepublishing.com
www.tuttlepublishing.com

Japan
Tuttle Publishing
Yaekari Building, 3rd Floor
5-4-12 Osaki
Shinagawa-ku
Tokyo 141 0032
Tel: (81) 3 5437-0171
Fax: (81) 3 5437-0755
sales@tuttle.co.jp
www.tuttle.co.jp

Asia Pacific
Berkeley Books Pte. Ltd.
3 Kallang Sector #04-01
Singapore 349278
Tel: (65) 6741-2178
Fax: (65) 6741-2179
inquiries@periplus.com.sg
www.tuttlepublishing.com

First edition
28 27 26 25 24   12 11 10 9 8   2401EP   Printed in China

TUTTLE PUBLISHING® is a registered trademark of Tuttle Publishing, a division of Periplus Editions (HK) Ltd.

Acknowledgments

There are many people I would like to acknowledge for the help they have given me in my practice. If I listed everyone, it would take many pages.

All of those with whom I have had the pleasure of practicing — from those with white belts to those with black belts, from the Brazilians to the foreigners — have in some way helped me with my unending search to improve my technique. They have helped me on my way through a complex martial art which is difficult to understand. It demands years of devotion to attain an upper level of maturity, as well as technical and pedagogical expertise.

I am convinced that it is not enough to gain knowledge; one must also know how to convey knowledge.

There are a few people that I need mention, however, as they have been present througout my life:

My friend and teacher **Romero Cavalcante, Jacare**, who opened my eyes to the sport. He is an example of how to combine the profesional career of a fighter and teacher with one's personal life, of how to transform a profession into a lifestyle and to enjoy what you are doing. I met so many friends in his school, not to mention Daniela, who became my wife.

My mother **Salvia**, who always understood and respected my will to do what I want. This allowed me to devote my efforts entirely to my practice.

My wife **Daniela:** a great athlete with international recognition, a black belt owner, and a cyclist who won the Race Across America 2009. She has sport in her blood. She is my greatest motivator who helped me discover new dimensions in sports, and who gave me beautiful children and a fantastic family.

My children, **Victorio**, **Julia**, and **Antonio**, for understanding my absence at home and for being aware of my love, a love that is bigger than any possible physical distance between us.

Fabio Gurgel, my great friend and colleague from the Alliance Team — a person with great character and excellent technique — who has always supported me. He is one of the best entrepreneurs in the martial arts world, one who has become an example for me.

Fernando Gurgel, Fabia's brother and my friend since the age of 3. He has always been like a brother to me. One of the best teachers in the academy.

Orlando Cani, my teacher and yoga master, a wonderful person who has enriched me with his friendship and respect. He is one of those people who is born to set an example of what it means to be a human.

Elcio Figueiredo, my long time friend and brother who, at the beginning of my teaching career, gave me strength. Although now we are far away from each other, he will always remain my oldest brother.

Luis Fernando , like a father to me, always sharing his precious advice and wisdom of the life of athlete.

Sebastian Slowek, my student and friend who is responsible for shaping up this book.

Markku Juntunen, who always comes to my mind when I think of a charismatic person from the martial arts world. He is also a true example of a great student and friend.

Alexandre Puga, my student and friend who works with me at the academy, always supporting me, always ready to help.

I would also like to acknowledge the Gracie Family for their input into the development of the exeptional martial art that Jiu-Jitsu is. I would especially like to mention:

Rickson Gracie, a warrior and an idol who inspired me and my generation. I have been honored with the privilege of practicing with him and being thought of by him.

I couldn't miss this opportunity to express my appreciation to those who were not a part of my sport's life, yet played imoprtant roles in my life in other ways.

Life's secret wisdom is to face every day of your life as if it were your last, trying to be the best possible human, not showing off in front of others, but merely for the sake of doing the best you can.

This type of thinking I owe my uncle Silvio, uncle Paulo, my cousin Marcinho, Davidowi Isaac (Mumm-Rá), my brother Kiko, Gilberto (Giba), Jules Sideratos, and my father Aldo Genovesi, who even though he wasn't able to assist me in my sporting career and did not see my children grow up, has always been a point of reference for me in both my good decisions and my mistakes.

As my mother-in-law used to say: "...the world is only for a few, for a very few." Life is in ours hands. We do not have to understand this fact to live in a happines which comes from what we have, not from what we have lost.

—Alexandre Paiva Genovesi

History of My Path in Jiu-Jitsu

I started Jiu-Jitsu practice in 1984 when I was 10 yeras old. Sergio Lauro Jardim, more commonly known as Malibu, encouraged me to take my first lesson in the Jacare shool where he taught some classes. Like any other teenager, I loved action movies and wanted to be a warrior, so the opportunity sounded perfect to me, almost like a dream come true. I always admired the advanced students, wondering if one day I would know what they know, and be able to perform what they can. Many things happened in those days, things which shaped me for the rest of my life.

In the beginning I devoted myself to pratice. But later, I had to face my greatest decision: whether I should follow my dreams and do what I really enjoy in my life, or choose something that would build my social position — a way of submitting to the rules of the market place (which was something I was expected to do).

My father's death was a shock, leaving me with great grief and a big, empty hole in my heart. Since then, I have had to be responsible for my family without having the support of somebody who could guide me. While death is a part of life, and does not have to set us back, this death was not expected. Many responsibilities and duties fell on my shoulders.

Another important moment came with my decision to get married and become a father. It is not an easy task to be a husband, a father, a teacher, and a warrior at the same time. Such a life instantly becomes busy with many responsibilities, and there is little time for fun. I think I am truly blessed with my job, which brings me joy and satisfaction.

When I injured my back in 1988, I was forced to stop practicing and wasn't able to see my friends. I wanted to be far away from the places and people I love so much. I thought I would not be able to resume my practice.

After surgery at the end of 1989, I began training again. I got my black belt in 1991. Then, in 1998, I went to a doctor to confirm what sort of exercises I could be doing to stay in top shape for an upcoming competition without hurting myself. I had been geting back injuries often. My doctor told me that I shouldn't practice at all, that I shouldn't involve myself in any serious sports or demanding activities. And especially, I shouldn't practice Jiu-Jitsu. I thought my life had ended, that my dreams were over.

I went to another doctor, my friend, who had taken care of me since my childhood. He decided that my condition was stable enough to not only practice, but also to participate in a competition (indicating that I should always be aware of the limitations, pain, and ailments I can experience at any time).

I felt confident. In 1999 I won all the competitions in which I participated, but a week before the world championships I sustained a bad knee injury. I went to my doctor, who assured me that he could perform surgery the same day. I had two options: either arthroscopy, to remove a piece of the meniscus, which would immobilze my knee; or normal surgery, in which a block would be placed into my knee, though without a warranty that at any moment it might not slip out of place. I chose the second option. I rested till the end of the week only to discover two days before the competition that I had gained some weight and needed to lose 8 kilograms in order to be able to compete in my weight category. The enormous weight gain was caused by a combination of two factors: medication containing corticosteroids placed in my knee, thus causing water retention, and the fact that my body was being deprived of high-energy activities. I lost the surplus weight, passed the weight test, and after surmounting uncountable obstacles and challenges, manged to reach my goal – I won the world championship.

All the obstacles I faced through the whole advanture, like the doctors diagnosing that I was almost handicapped, only made my sucess taste sweeter and more satisfying.

The Alliance Academy was created in 1994 from the joint forces of the Master Academy (Jacare and Fabio Gurgel) and Strike (my school in those days). We didn't want our teams competing with each other in prestigious domestic and international competitions.

Our decision to join forces and establish one strong tournament team with the potential to win was welcomed with interest — other schools joined the Alliance team and began competing under this name.

Currently the Alliance team is a four-time world championship winner (1999, 2000, 2008, 2009); the Panamerican championship winner in 2009; the Brazilian championship winner in 2009; and was choosen the best tournament team by many sides.

Alliance gave an opportunity to many great athletes including Leonardo Vieira, Leonardo Leite, Fernando Terere, Ricardo Vieira, Claudio Moreno, Marcos Meireles, Alexandre Street, Gabriel Leite, Marcelo Garcia, Alex Monsalve, Lucas Lepre, Michael Langhi, Cobrinha, Sergio Moraes, Damien Maia, and many others.

Jiu-jitsu

Jiu-Jitsu techniques can be characterized by a reasoning process similar to the one found in the game of chess. In both activities, all actions are defined by logic, tactics and strategy.

Your path in Jiu-Jitsu can be compared to attempting to solve a puzzle. At the beginning, we are given a few elements that are easy enough to figure out. As soon as we solve the easy ones, however, we are facing a more complicated puzzle, with more elements to piece together. It is hard to imagine how many techniques are possible, how many techniques can be created. The variety of techniques can encourage one to not only know possitions, but to also try to understand the mechanics of movement.

The logic, tactics, and strategy in techniques must be built on the knowledge of anatomy. One must know body parts, structure, mechanics, and all kinds of limitations — the limitations of the range of motion needed to execute sprains and needed to perform chokes. Based of this sort of knowledge, one can learn how to use locks and pins to force the opponent into submission. This is a close contact fight, body to body. Both fighters need to set their own strategy and tactics of attack, but they also have to understand and anticipate the opponent's moves and possible actions in order to counteract.

Playing chess and practicing Jiu-Jitsu demand exercising the anticipation of the opponent's moves. Thus, playing chess might bring advantages for the Jiu-Jitsu student and can be a part of the learning process.

Beside its physical side, Jiu-Jitsu has also a moral and ethical context, which also gives students training in moral aspects. When practicing with a sense of proportion and respect for the opponent, Jiu-Jitsu is very positive and moral. Practicing with others allows one to develop friendships and to bond with other people. The social aspect keeps the student coming back, continuing to practice and — finally — achieving new skills. Jiu-Jitsu is a wonderful way to educate a person and allow them to develop social tools.

Without doubt, Jiu-Jitsu is an effective martial art. It has been proved as such in comparison with others martial techniques, and included in the training routines of those who fight the most brutal combat: World Vale Tudo Championship (WVC), Ultimate Fighting Championship (UFC), and Pride Fighting Championships (Pride FC). Being aware of Jiu-Jitsu's advantages and effectiveness helps students to develop self-confidence and self-esteem.

Technical development in Jiu-Jitsu depends on the way one maintains discipline in many aspects of daily life, such as a healthy diet, a regular schedule, etc. This discipline is another way of saying self-control.

The practice of martial arts is also a great life lesson which will prepare students to face their surrounding reality by teaching them about their limitations, increasing their self-esteem and confidence, and improving their motor skills. Practicing a martial art teaches one to respect one's friend and opponents, to handle both victory and failure.

If only we choose, we can live our dream life and achieve everything we want, instead of watching as time passes by. Jiu-Jitsu can be of great use in creating and preparing for such a life.

CHAPTER 1

Takedowns with GI

Koshiki Taoshi - Ouchi Gari

The left hand grabs the opponent's collar and stretches it out. This allows the right hand to grip more powerfully.

Right hand grabs the collar on side of the neck.

Pull the opponent towards you. He steps forward. Your left hand grabs his right hand to prevent an attack.

Your right foot hooks his right foot from the inside. He loses his balance. Your left hand grabs his knee from underneath.

Lift up the opponent's legs and then enter with your left foot forward.

Enter forward. Take down the opponent by scooping up his supporting leg.

Enter with hip. Your undercut is stronger and more effective when you use your hips to enter.

BRAZILIAN JIU-JITSU

Oushi Gari - Kibisu Gaeshi

Start by strongly gripping your opponent's collar. Drag him in and take his balance.

Pull your opponent towards you. Kneel down and forward. The heel (foot) scoops his leg from the inside.

While blocking his back leg, grab the ankle of his front leg.

Slam into him, then drive him to the ground. The right hand pushes him down to the ground while the left hand continues blocking his front leg.

Mount in the dominate position so you can finish the technique.

Sukui Nage

Grab the opponent's gi collar. While passing by him, rapidly pull him down.

Your left hand hooks underneath his right knee from the outside.

Turning and bringing down your body will force the opponent down. Mount in the dominate position.

Kibisu Gaeshi

Your left hand grabs the opponent's collar and stretches it out. This allows the right hand to grip more powerfully.

Pull the opponent towards you, forcing him to step forward. The left hand grabs the opponent's front ankle from the inside. The right hand keeps him straight and unable to bend over.

While lifting his leg up, straighten you right arm, taking his balance.

With your right foot hook his supporting leg's ankle and turn your body.

After putting the opponent on the ground, you can fully control him and finish with the appropriate techinque.

By cutting down your opponent's supporting leg and twisting your body around, you can knock him over

CHAPTER 2

The Closed Guard with Gi

BRAZILIAN JIU-JITSU

Arm bar from the closed guard

Closed guard. Lock your opponent's left hand. Your right hand grabs his lapel and your right foot rests on his hip .

Press your left leg against your opponent's right side. Put your right leg on his left shoulder. Use your hands to pull him down to you.

Move your right leg over your opponent's head. Press his neck with the calf of your right leg. Raise your hips. Your opponent should tap out.

DANGEROUS TECHNIQUE • BEWARE •

Your right hand, which is holding the opponent's collar, moves up and pushes his head to the side.

Choke from the closed guard

Closed guard. Your left hand grabs his collar and pulls it out. Get a deep collar grip with your right hand.

DANGEROUS TECHNIQUE • BEWARE •

Reaching closely across the opponent's body, use your left hand to grip his gi collar on the right side.

Pull both of your hands simultaneously to your body. Your opponent is locked against you, choked.

You can increase the choking pressure by twisting your body to the right.

BRAZILIAN JIU-JITSU

Closed guard sweep to back control

Closed guard. Your left hand holds the left sleeve of the opponent's gi. With the right hand grab the same (left) sleeve by the elbow. Use both your hands to shove the opponent's arm towards you and aside.

Lift up your hips and thrust them forward. Your right hand grabs opponent's right shoulder and pulls him backwards.

Your left hand grabs the opponent's right leg by his gi pants. Your right hand is still gripping his right shoulder.

Pull opponent's right shoulder back and thrust your left hip forward. Roll over to your right side. Rotate.

Rotate your body. Cross-pass the opponent's right leg. Shove his right shoulder back and thrust your hips forward.

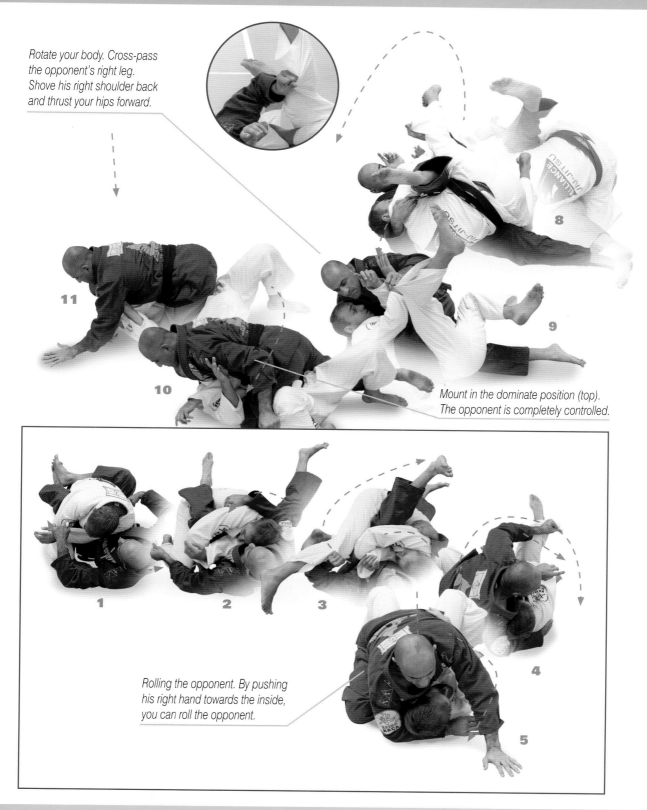

Mount in the dominate position (top). The opponent is completely controlled.

Rolling the opponent. By pushing his right hand towards the inside, you can roll the opponent.

BRAZILIAN JIU-JITSU

Umaplata sweep from arm bar in the closed guard

Lock the opponent in the closed guard. Grab the right sleeve of his gi.

The closed guard. Hook your left hand underneath the opponent's right knee from inside.

DANGEROUS TECHNIQUE • BEWARE •

Lock the opponent's right arm and thrust your hips forward.

Straighten the opponent's right leg, lock it, then pull his right hand to his locked right leg. Pull his left arm toward you. Move your right leg over his neck.

Collar choke from the closed guard with one arm trapped

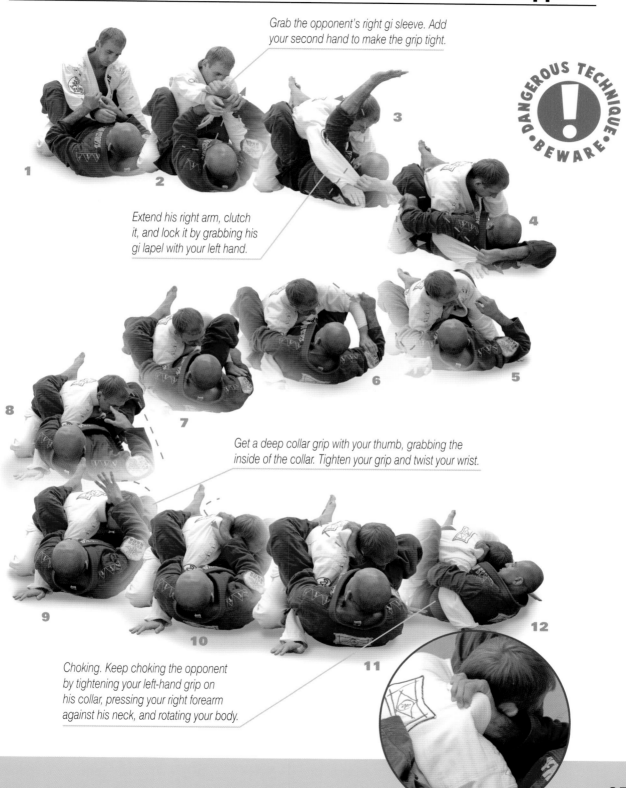

Grab the opponent's right gi sleeve. Add your second hand to make the grip tight.

Extend his right arm, clutch it, and lock it by grabbing his gi lapel with your left hand.

Get a deep collar grip with your thumb, grabbing the inside of the collar. Tighten your grip and twist your wrist.

Choking. Keep choking the opponent by tightening your left-hand grip on his collar, pressing your right forearm against his neck, and rotating your body.

DANGEROUS TECHNIQUE · BEWARE ·

BRAZILIAN JIU-JITSU

Sweep to mount from the closed guard

The closed guard. Hook your left hand underneath the opponent's right knee from inside.

Straighten his leg and then lock it. Drag his right hand toward his locked leg.

Lock his right hand and thrust your hips foward. Roll your body to the left and start rotation.

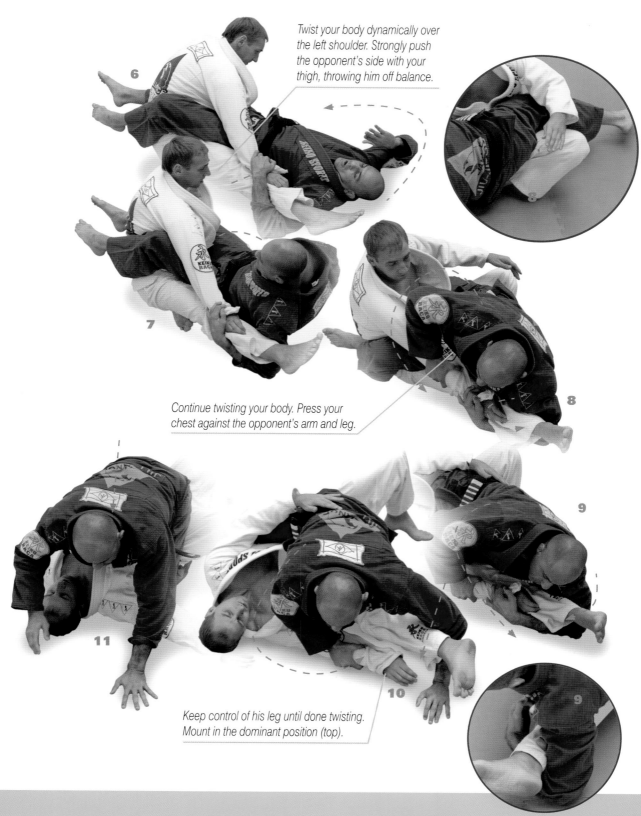

Twist your body dynamically over the left shoulder. Strongly push the opponent's side with your thigh, throwing him off balance.

Continue twisting your body. Press your chest against the opponent's arm and leg.

Keep control of his leg until done twisting. Mount in the dominant position (top).

BRAZILIAN JIU-JITSU

Arm bar from the close guard with your opponent's arm trapped

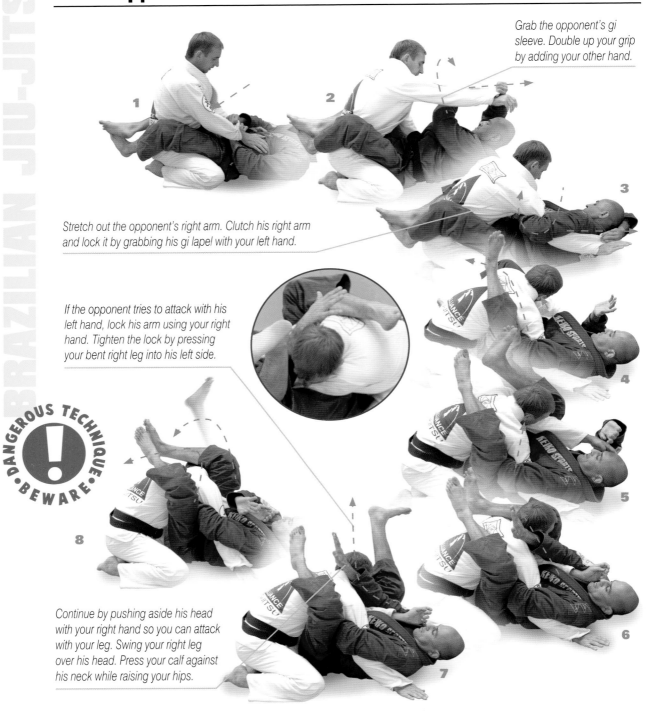

Grab the opponent's gi sleeve. Double up your grip by adding your other hand.

Stretch out the opponent's right arm. Clutch his right arm and lock it by grabbing his gi lapel with your left hand.

If the opponent tries to attack with his left hand, lock his arm using your right hand. Tighten the lock by pressing your bent right leg into his left side.

DANGEROUS TECHNIQUE · BEWARE ·

Continue by pushing aside his head with your right hand so you can attack with your leg. Swing your right leg over his head. Press your calf against his neck while raising your hips.

Sweep to mount from the closed guard when your opponent stands

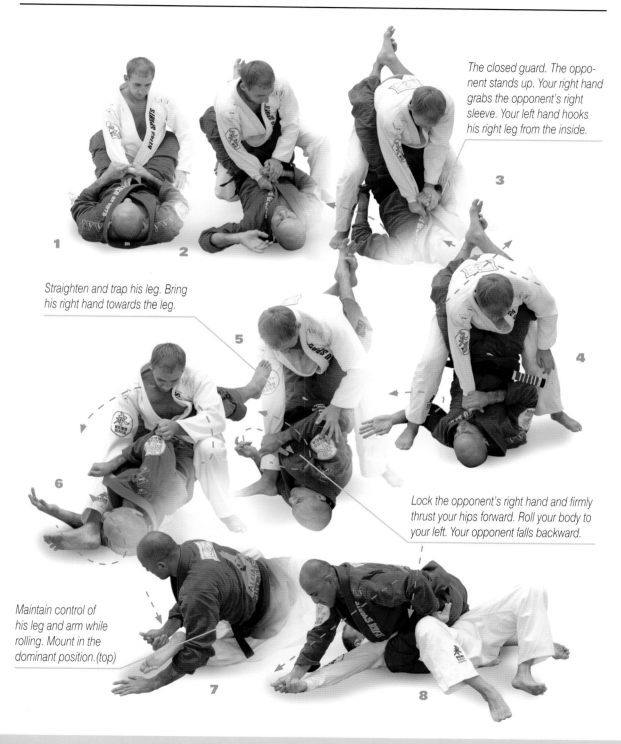

The closed guard. The opponent stands up. Your right hand grabs the opponent's right sleeve. Your left hand hooks his right leg from the inside.

Straighten and trap his leg. Bring his right hand towards the leg.

Lock the opponent's right hand and firmly thrust your hips forward. Roll your body to your left. Your opponent falls backward.

Maintain control of his leg and arm while rolling. Mount in the dominant position. (top)

Sweep from Umaplata when your opponent stands

The closed guard. The opponent stands up. Your right hand grabs the opponent's right sleeve. Your left hand hooks his right leg from the inside.

Swivel your body to the left so your head is close to opponent's right leg. Lunge with your right leg.

Straighten and trap the opponent's right leg while shoving his right hand towards the leg.

Lock his right elbow and press with your legs against his arm. Turn your body and start rolling over your right shoulder.

Rolling. Keep opponent's right arm and leg locked.

Hook under the opponent's right knee and fold his right leg over his left knee. Slide your hips forward, dig your right knee into his rib cage. The dominant side position.

Umaplata from arm bar in the closed guard

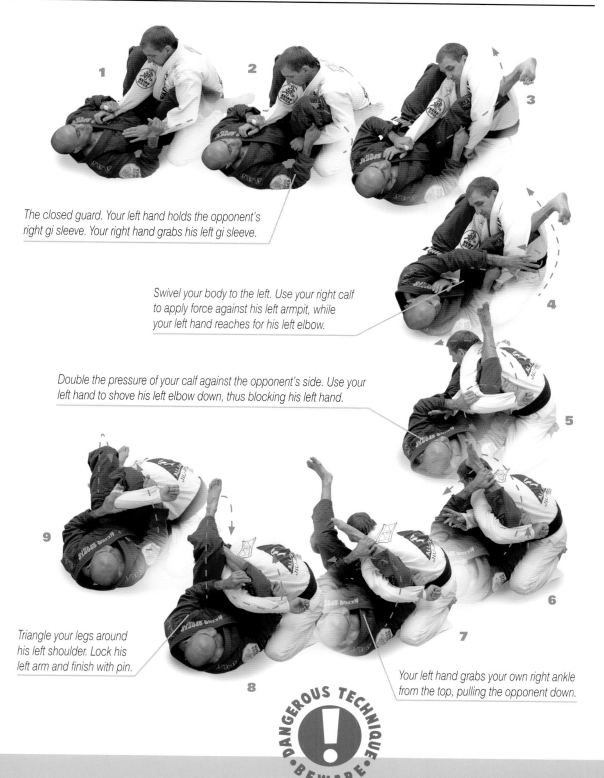

The closed guard. Your left hand holds the opponent's right gi sleeve. Your right hand grabs his left gi sleeve.

Swivel your body to the left. Use your right calf to apply force against his left armpit, while your left hand reaches for his left elbow.

Double the pressure of your calf against the opponent's side. Use your left hand to shove his left elbow down, thus blocking his left hand.

Triangle your legs around his left shoulder. Lock his left arm and finish with pin.

Your left hand grabs your own right ankle from the top, pulling the opponent down.

Arm bar from the closed guard when your opponent stands

You opponent stands up, attempting to get out of your closed guard. Slide your crossed legs along the opponent's back, towards his shoulder blades.

While swiveling your body to the left, your right hand blocks the opponent's leg from inside. Your left hand holds down his right hand.

Swing your left leg over the opponent's head. Thrust your hips forward. Press your calf against his neck.

Release the lock. Lower your hips. The opposite side is being attacked. Repeat the entire sequence in the same order.

DANGEROUS TECHNIQUE · BEWARE ·

Close guard sweep to mount from the kimura position

The closed guard. Place your left hand on the mat to help you shift your hips forward. Use your right hand either to grab the back of your opponent's gi or his gi belt.

Strongly thrust your hips forward. Use your right hand to reach out to his right elbow. Press your right thigh against his body.

Firmly turn your body and tightly grab your opponent's arm. Thrust your right hip forward.

Mount in the dominant position (top). Your opponent is completely controlled.

BRAZILIAN JIU-JITSU

Kimura from the closed guard

The closed guard position. Raise your body up on your left elbow. Your left hand grabs the opponent's right wrist. Your right arm circles over his head to wrap around his right arm.

Thrust your hips forward. Your right arm slides under the opponent's right elbow and grabs your left hand wrist from the top.

DANGEROUS TECHNIQUE • BEWARE •

Force his folded arm up his back. By swiveling your body you are tightening the lock.

Guillotine from the closed guard

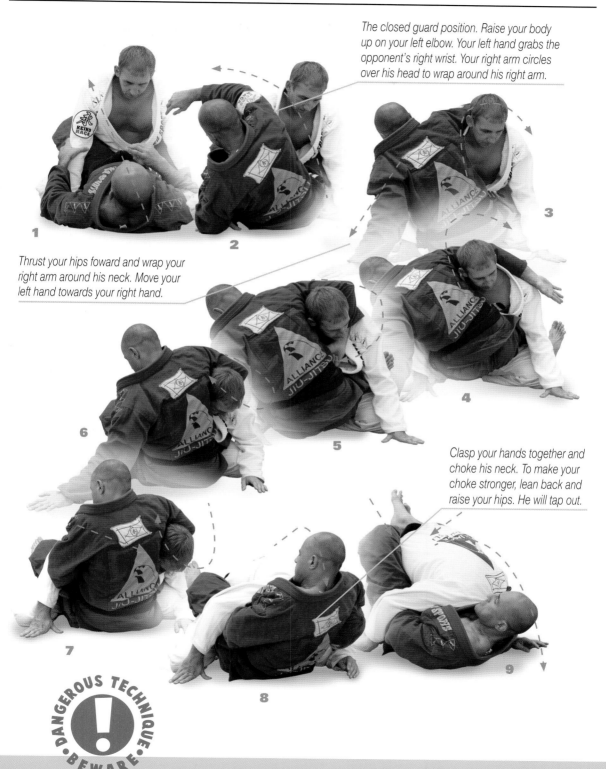

The closed guard position. Raise your body up on your left elbow. Your left hand grabs the opponent's right wrist. Your right arm circles over his head to wrap around his right arm.

Thrust your hips foward and wrap your right arm around his neck. Move your left hand towards your right hand.

Clasp your hands together and choke his neck. To make your choke stronger, lean back and raise your hips. He will tap out.

DANGEROUS TECHNIQUE • BEWARE •

CHAPTER 3

Passing the Closed Guard with Gi

Passing the closed guard

Your opponent is in the closed guard position. Grab the front of his gi with your right hand. With your left hand seize the opponent's gi on his left hip.

Stand up. Jab his inner thigh with your left elbow.

Push the opponent's right leg down. Use your right arm to block his left leg from the outside.

Press your right shoulder against his thigh. Grab his gi pants with your left hand.

Use your left hand to shove him on to his side, then on to his back.

Passing the high closed guard securing one sleeve

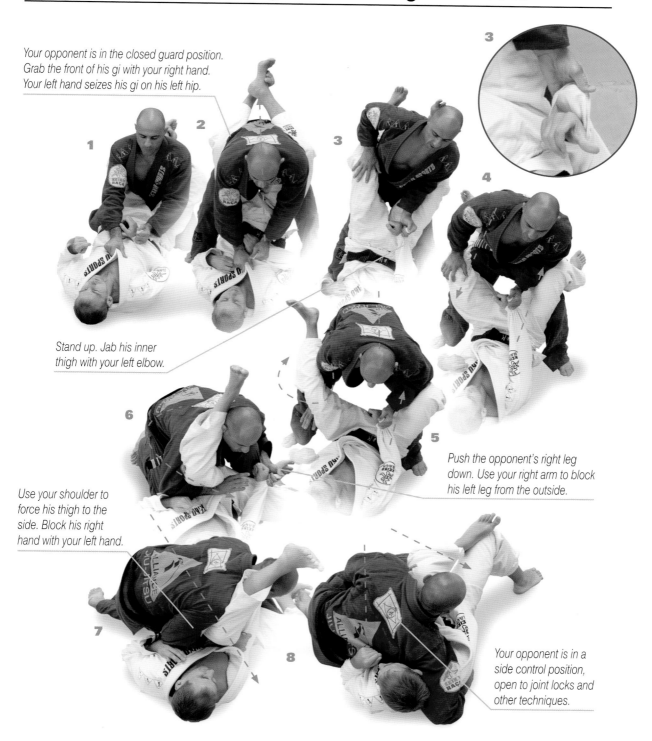

Your opponent is in the closed guard position. Grab the front of his gi with your right hand. Your left hand seizes his gi on his left hip.

Stand up. Jab his inner thigh with your left elbow.

Push the opponent's right leg down. Use your right arm to block his left leg from the outside.

Use your shoulder to force his thigh to the side. Block his right hand with your left hand.

Your opponent is in a side control position, open to joint locks and other techniques.

Passing the high closed guard gripping your opponent's collar

Your opponent is in the closed guard position. Grab his collar firmly with both hands. Stand up and haul the opponent up. Your hands are gripping his collar.

Stand-up position. Your opponent is in the closed guard position.

Your left hand pushes down strongly against the inner part of the opponent's left thigh.

Break the guard. Push his right leg down. He falls down on his back.

Press your shin against opponent's right thigh.
Your right hand blocks his left leg from the inside.

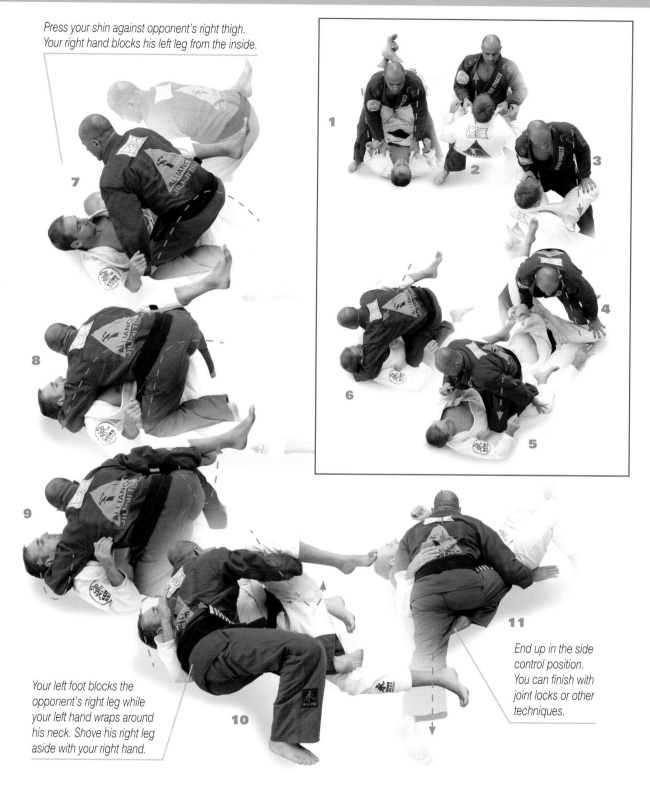

Your left foot blocks the
opponent's right leg while
your left hand wraps around
his neck. Shove his right leg
aside with your right hand.

End up in the side
control position.
You can finish with
joint locks or other
techniques.

Passing the guard controlling your opponent's arm

The opponent is in the closed guard position. Your right hand grabs the front of his gi. Your left hand grips his right sleeve.

When the opponent attempts to reach for your gi's left collar with his left hand, grab his left wrist, then shove his arm down and straighten it out.

Stand up. Shove opponent's left leg down using your right hand. Your second hand grips his left sleeve.

Break your opponent's guard and kneel down, placing your right knee just behind his thigh. Your left hand holds his left hand.

Passing the low closed guard while holding your opponent's wrist

The opponent is in the closed guard position. Grab his right wrist with your left hand. Your right hand grips his gi lapel.

Lunge forward. Straighten and spread your legs, forcing his right hand under his lower back.

Your right hand catches the opponent's right hand behind his back.

Slide your left leg out from the guard position. Shove your hips forward. Now slide your right leg out from the guard. Mount in dominant position.

Push your opponent's right leg down to the mat with your left hand. Your second hand continues to hold his right hand behind his back.

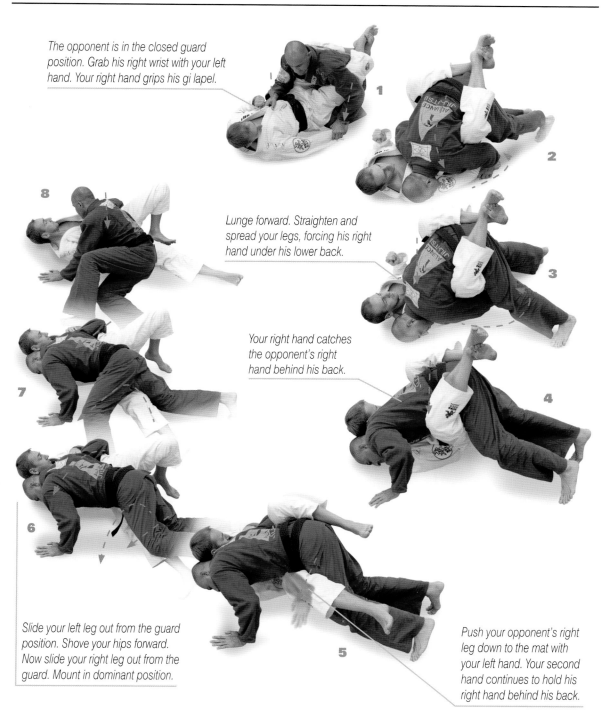

CHAPTER 4

Butterfly guard and X-guard with Gi

Butterfly guard sweep

The butterfly guard position. Place your right hand behind your opponent's back, pressing his left arm. Bend your right leg, leaving your feet beneath his left thigh.

Simultaneously kick your opponent's left thigh up with your right foot while pivoting your body dynamically to the left. Your left hand pulls his body down and to the left, while your right hands pushes it up and to the left.

Keep turning your body. Jab your knee into his belly, then switch to the mount position. End up in the dominant position (top).

Butterfly guard sweep gripping your opponent's belt

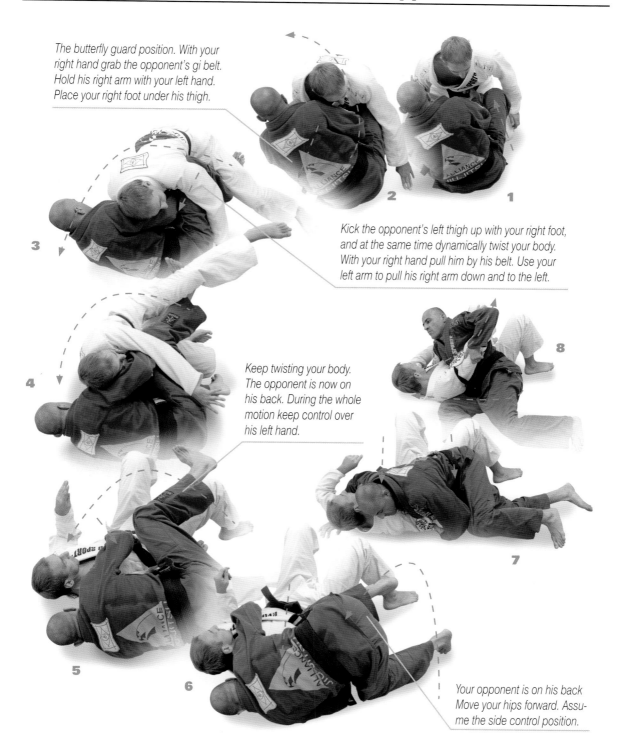

The butterfly guard position. With your right hand grab the opponent's gi belt. Hold his right arm with your left hand. Place your right foot under his thigh.

Kick the opponent's left thigh up with your right foot, and at the same time dynamically twist your body. With your right hand pull him by his belt. Use your left arm to pull his right arm down and to the left.

Keep twisting your body. The opponent is now on his back. During the whole motion keep control over his left hand.

Your opponent is on his back Move your hips forward. Assume the side control position.

BRAZILIAN JIU-JITSU

Butterfly guard sweep to back control

Force your opponent's left thigh up with your right foot, and at the same time twist your body. Place your right hand on his back and tug his gi. Your left hand holds and blocks his right arm.

Your left hand drives his right arm up. Drive your head under your opponent's shoulder, keeping it close to his body. Toss his body up in the air and pull your hips back. He lands on his side.

Wrap your left hand around your opponent's neck. Add the other hand and choke him. At the same time triangle your legs around his hips and thighs.

Force your opponent's left thigh up with your right foot while twisting your body. Place your right hand on his back and tug his gi. Your left hand holds and blocks your opponent's right arm.

Butterfly guard sweep holding a leg and arm and standing up

Force your opponent's left thigh up with your right foot. Place your right hand on his back and tug his gi. Your left hand holds and blocks your opponent's right arm.

Your left arm hooks his right leg from underneath. Bring his leg towards your shoulder.

Slide your body back and straighten his leg. Place his leg on your shoulder.

Thrust your body forward and up, keeping the opponent's leg on your shoulder.

Butterfly sweep holding a leg and arm to side control

Force your opponent's left thigh up with your right foot. Place your right hand on his back and tug his gi. Your left hand holds and blocks his right arm.

Your left arm hooks the opponent's right leg from underneath. Bring his leg towards your shoulder.

Push your opponent backwards. His leg rests on your sholder. Roll him onto his back.

Butterfly guard transition to X-guard sweep to the front of your opponent

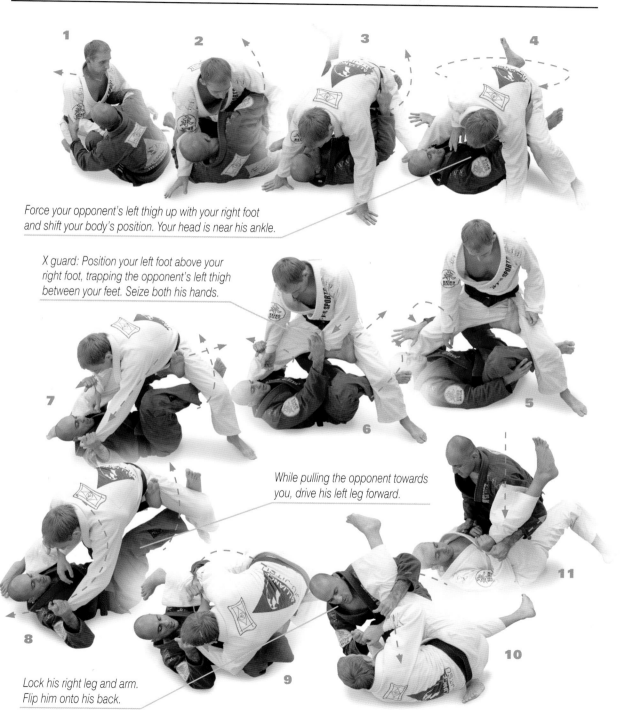

Force your opponent's left thigh up with your right foot and shift your body's position. Your head is near his ankle.

X guard: Position your left foot above your right foot, trapping the opponent's left thigh between your feet. Seize both his hands.

While pulling the opponent towards you, drive his left leg forward.

Lock his right leg and arm. Flip him onto his back.

Butterfly guard sweep to technical stand up

Force your opponent's left thigh up with your right foot. Place your right hand on his back and tug his gi. Your left hand holds and blocks his right arm.

Use your left leg to push his right leg towards your body. At the same time grab underneath his left leg with your left hand and bring the leg toward your shoulder.

Move your body back and straighten his leg. Rest his leg on your shoulder.

Block your opponent's left thigh with your right foot.

9

10

11

12

Step back and stand up. His leg remains on your shoulder.

13

14

8

Block the opponent's leg, step back, and stand up.

9

11

15

Grab his belt and turn him over onto his back. End up in the dominant position.

Butterfly guard transition to X-guard sweep to the back of your opponent

Force your opponent's left thigh up with your right foot and shift your body's position. Your head is near his ankle.

While pulling the opponent towards you, drive his left leg forward.

X guard: Position your left foot above your right foot, trapping the opponent's left thigh between your feet. Seize both his hands.

The opponent's right hand and leg are locked. Hook your right leg under his left knee and flip him onto his back.

Spider guard sweep to back control

Block the opponent's right hand by pushing his arm up with your left leg while holding his sleeve with your left hand. Grab his gi lapel with your right hand.

At the same time you are shoving the opponent's right arm up with your left leg, force his right thigh up, and rotate your torso underneath his left leg.

Scoot underneath your oppponent. Trap his right thigh between your legs. With your right hand, grab his gi belt on his back and pull him down.

Using the grip on the belt pull him down. Kick his right leg up. He falls down onto his back.

Spider Guard sweep with a hook while holding your opponent's ankle

Spider Guard position. The opponent's right arm is blocked by pushing it up with your leg while holding the right sleeve with the left hand. The right hand grasps his lapel.

In one instant use your left leg to push the opponent's right arm upwards, force his right thigh up, and pull his lapel with your right hand.

Push him up to the standing position.

Swivel your body toward your opponent's left leg. His arms and right leg are locked in the guard.

Let go of his lapel and with your right hand grab his right ankle.

Rotate your body and press the opponent forward. Your right leg presses under his right thigh. Pull him down with your left hand.

Your opponent falls onto his back. His right hand and right leg are still under your control.

End up in the dominant position with full control over your opponent.

CHAPTER 5

Open Guard Pass with Gi

Open guard pass controlling the hips

With both hands grab your opponent's gi pants at the knees.

With your left hand push his right leg to the outside. Step forward and stick your knee into his thigh.

Press your shoulder against your opponent's thigh. Place your arm around his waist, grabbing his belt with your right hand.

Hook your right hand under his right leg and shove the leg aside.

Press the weight of your body onto him and shove his hips aside.

Flip him onto his back. End up in the side control position.

The "Bullfighter" open guard pass

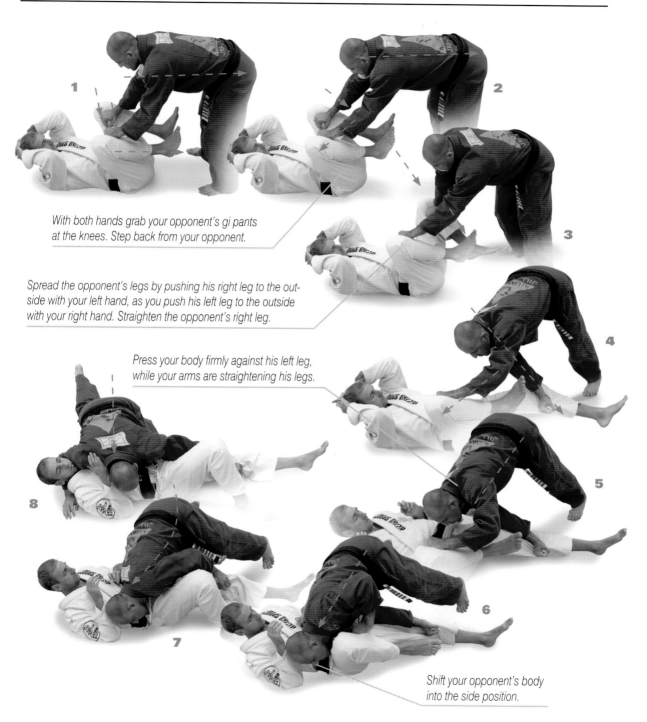

With both hands grab your opponent's gi pants at the knees. Step back from your opponent.

Spread the opponent's legs by pushing his right leg to the outside with your left hand, as you push his left leg to the outside with your right hand. Straighten the opponent's right leg.

Press your body firmly against his left leg, while your arms are straightening his legs.

Shift your opponent's body into the side position.

Knee cut across open guard pass

With both hands grab your opponent's gi pants at the knees. Push his right leg to the outside. Step forward and stick your knee into his thigh.

Block his right thigh with your right knee. Seize his right arm.

Press your body against his body and stretch out his left arm.

Switch the position of your legs. With your opponent lying on his back, switch into the side position.

Knee cut across open guard pass when the opponent blocks with his leg

With both hands grab your opponent's gi pants at the knees. Push his right leg to the outside. Step forward and stick your knee into his thigh.

Block his right thigh with your right knee. Use your arm to shove his left leg down.

Hook your right arm underneath your opponent's right knee.

Press your body against his body. Seize his gi lapel.

Switch the position of your legs. With your opponent lying on his back, switch into the side position.

CHAPTER 6

Across-side Position with Gi

Armbar from side control

Start from the dominant side position. Move around your opponent's head.

Seize your opponent's left arm. Double the strength of your grip by adding a second hand

Drag your opponent's arm up. Move your leg over his head. Lean back.

Stretch out and straighten while still bending your opponent's arm. Apply armbar joint lock.

DANGEROUS TECH • BEWARE

Kimura from the north-south position

Start from the dominant side position. Move around your opponent's head.

Trap the opponent's head between your knees. Use your left arm to seize his left arm. Straighten the arm out and block it.

Seize the top of his left forearm with your right hand. Double the grip by adding your left hand.

Stretch out your opponent's arm. Swing your leg over his head. Twist your body towards your left leg.

DANGEROUS TECHNIQUE · BEWARE ·

Kimura to choke from the north-south position

Start from the dominant side position. Move around your opponent's head.

Trap your opponent's head between your knees. With your left arm, seize and block his left arm.

Grip his gi belt or hem of his gi with your left hand. Block his left forearm. Seize your opponent's gi lapel with your right hand, and swing your right leg over his head. Press your right forearm against his throat.

DANGEROUS TECHNIQUE · BEWARE ·

Armbar from side control to the other side

The dominant side position. Block your opponent's left arm.

Seize your opponent's left arm just above his elbow.

Press against his neck with your left hand. Move your left foot over his head.

DANGEROUS TECHNIQUE • BEWARE •

Shift your position by rotating your body over your opponent. Grab his left leg by his gi pants. Straighten and extend his left arm. Apply armbar joint lock.

Choke from side control with the arm trapped

The dominant side position. Walk around your opponent's head.

Grab his gi collar with your left hand, then shift the collar grip to your right hand. Stretch your right arm out as far as possible.

Grab your opponent's gi collar with your left hand. Move your right leg back, behind his head. Press your right forearm against his throat. While the left hand grabs his gi collar, your left leg blocks his head.

DANGEROUS TECHNIQUE • BEWARE •

North-south choke

The dominant position. Move around your opponent's head.

Grab his gi collar with your left hand, then shift the collar grip to your right hand. Use your right hand to stretch his collar out.

Rotate your right arm, pointing your elbow towards you. Press your forearm against his throat.

DANGEROUS TECHNIQUE • BEWARE •

Choke from side control

The side control dominant position. Your right arm wraps around the opponent's waist. Your left arm slides underneath his neck and grabs his collar.

1

Stretch your opponent's collar out with your left hand. Move your right hand towards your left hand.

2

Switch your grip. Now your right hand grabs the back of your opponent's collar. Your left hand seizes his front collar while you press your forearm against his throat.

6

3

5

4

DANGEROUS TECHNIQUE · BEWARE ·

Choke from side control with hand on collar similiar to Katagatame

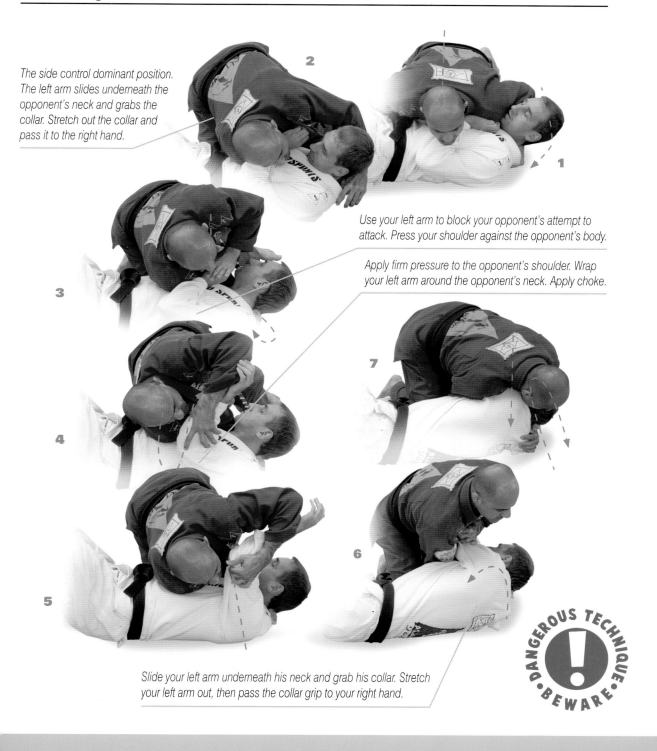

The side control dominant position. The left arm slides underneath the opponent's neck and grabs the collar. Stretch out the collar and pass it to the right hand.

Use your left arm to block your opponent's attempt to attack. Press your shoulder against the opponent's body.

Apply firm pressure to the opponent's shoulder. Wrap your left arm around the opponent's neck. Apply choke.

Slide your left arm underneath his neck and grab his collar. Stretch your left arm out, then pass the collar grip to your right hand.

DANGEROUS TECHNIQUE • BEWARE •

Mount sliding knee to belly

The side control dominant position. Slide your left arm under his head while sliding your right hand under his left elbow. Clasp your hands together.

Use your right knee to shove your opponent's right knee aside. The opponent is now on his side.

Thrust your body forward. Trap your opponent in a firm grip. Jab your knee against his right hip.

Open your opponent's position by thrusting your hips forward and pressing with your right arm against his left. Put your leg over your opponent and enter the mount position.

Arm bar from the mount

The dominant position – the mount, top.
Left arm behind the opponent's head. Wedge both knees under his armpits. Your opponent covers himself with his left hand while attempting to shove you off.

Your right arm is tightening and pressing the opponent's elbow until the moment your left hand can grab your right hand.

Bring your left knee over your opponent's right arm.

Pull up and tighten the grip over the opponent's head and arm. Set your right leg on the mat.

Move your right leg over his head. Unbend your opponent's arm and stretch it out. Apply the armbar joint lock.

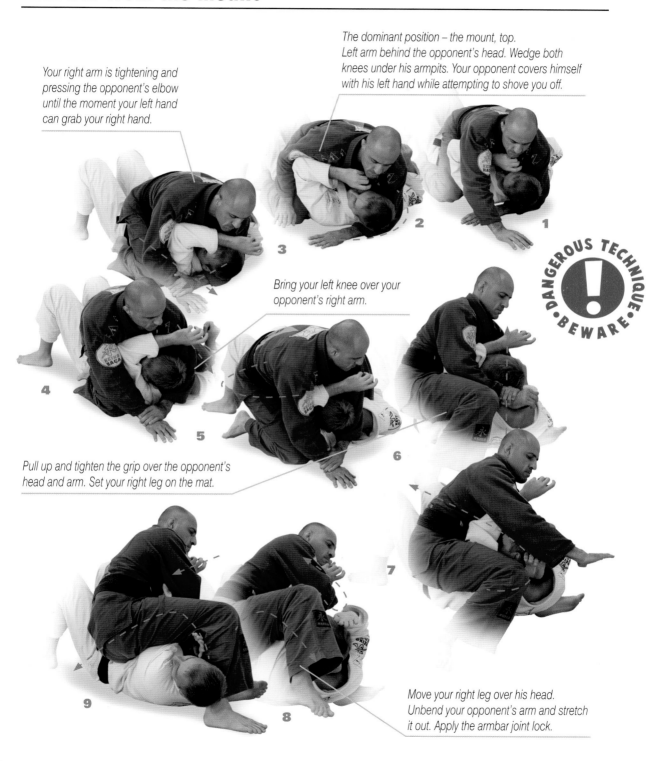

BRAZILIAN JIU-JITSU

Arm bar from te mount in both arms

Swing your hips and shift to the opposite side of the opponent. Pull out his bent left arm.

The opponent tangles his arms, making it impossible to apply the lock.

Move your leg over the opponent's head. Pull his bent arm up and straighten both his arms.

DANGEROUS TECHNIQUE • BEWARE •

Pull his bent arm up, extending it while leaning back. Apply the armbar joint lock.

(Different angle)

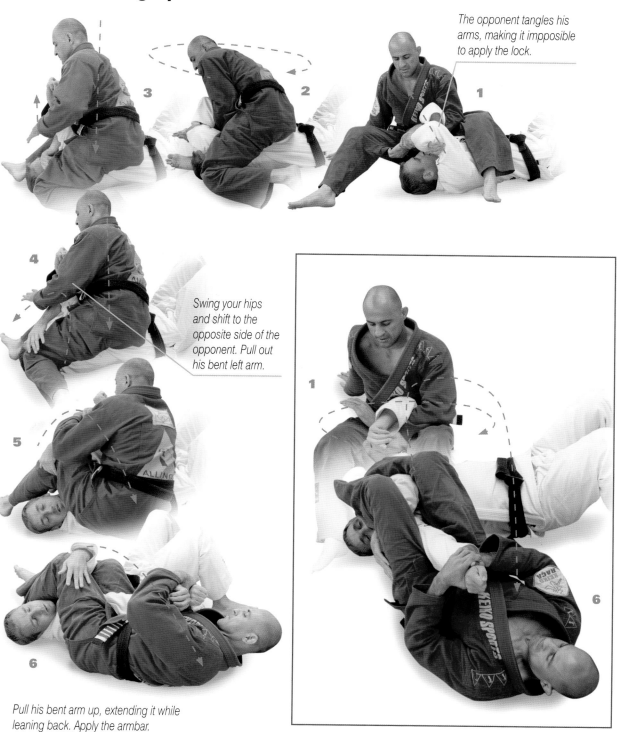

The opponent tangles his arms, making it impossible to apply the lock.

1

2

3

4

Swing your hips and shift to the opposite side of the opponent. Pull out his bent left arm.

5

6

1

6

Pull his bent arm up, extending it while leaning back. Apply the armbar.

CHAPTER 7

Across-side Position with Gi

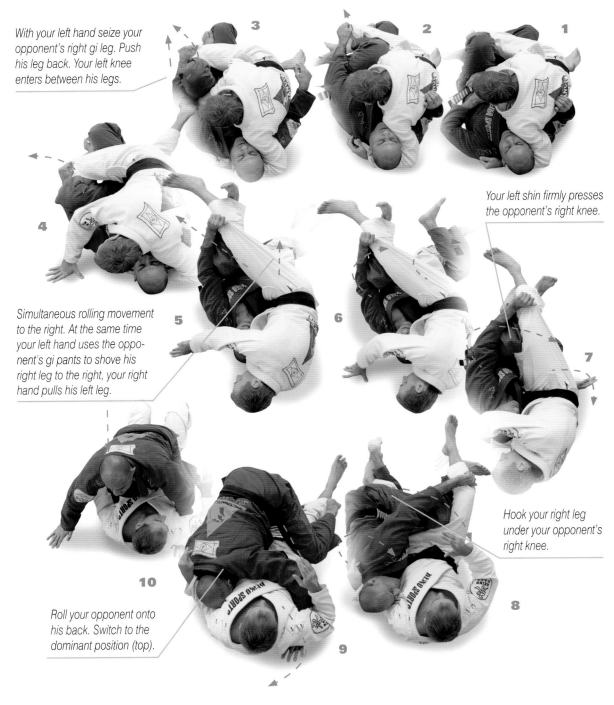

Half guard sweep to mount

With your left hand seize your opponent's right gi leg. Push his leg back. Your left knee enters between his legs.

Your left shin firmly presses the opponent's right knee.

Simultaneous rolling movement to the right. At the same time your left hand uses the opponent's gi pants to shove his right leg to the right, your right hand pulls his left leg.

Hook your right leg under your opponent's right knee.

Roll your opponent onto his back. Switch to the dominant position (top).

Recover close guard in half guard with hook

The opponent is held in half-guard. Your legs wrap around his right leg.

Grab the opponent's belt behind his back. Untangle your legs. Hook your left foot under your opponent's right knee and lift him up.

Your right hand grabs the opponent's left gi leg. Pull and force the leg up.

Spread your legs. The opponent falls between them. Close the guard.

Half guard sweep dominating your opponent's arm

The opponent is held in the half-guard. Your legs wrap around his right leg.

Rest your hand on his shoulder. Straighten your arm and shove your body back. Your leg stays set in half-guard.

Twist your body. Reach far behind your opponent's left shoulder with your left arm.

Press your left thigh against the opponent's hips. Turn your body towards his left arm. Rolling.

Half guard sweep dominating your opponent's legs

The opponent is held in the half-guard. Rest your hand on his shoulder. Straighten your arm and shove your body back. Your leg stays set in half-guard.

Swivel your body and dive under your opponent. Seize the opponent's gi collar.

Pass your grip on the opponent's collar from your left to right hand. Your right hand sweeps underneath the opponent's left calf.

Your left hand grabs his left ankle. Your right hand, which grabs the opponent's gi, helps to lock his left leg.

Twist your body and roll with your opponent towards the left. Block his right leg with your left leg.

Keep rolling. Flip the opponent onto his back. Maintain control of his left leg. Move to the side control position.

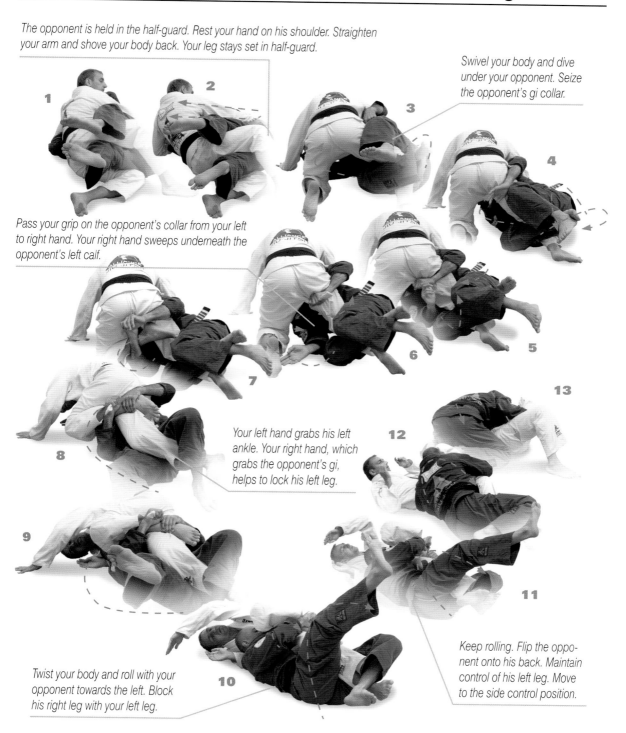

CHAPTER 8

Turtle Guard and Back Mount with Gi

BRAZILIAN JIU-JITSU

Turtle guard attack to taking the back with one leg over the shoulder

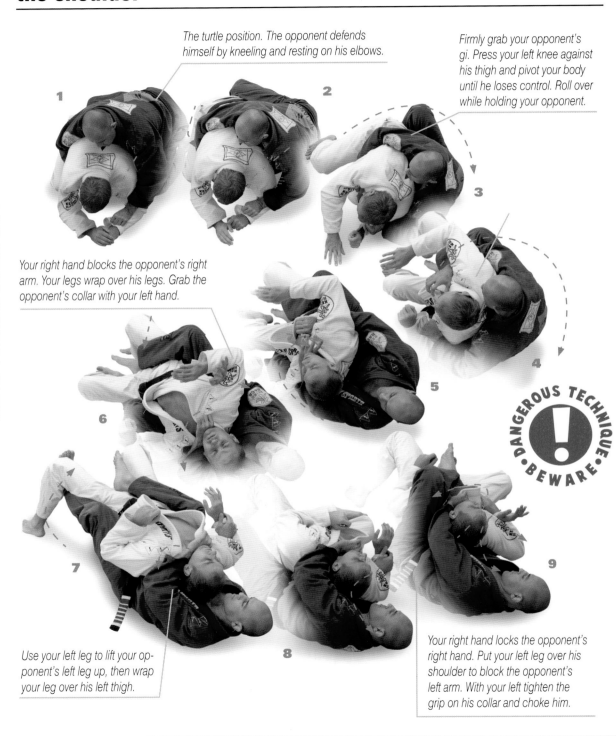

The turtle position. The opponent defends himself by kneeling and resting on his elbows.

Firmly grab your opponent's gi. Press your left knee against his thigh and pivot your body until he loses control. Roll over while holding your opponent.

Your right hand blocks the opponent's right arm. Your legs wrap over his legs. Grab the opponent's collar with your left hand.

DANGEROUS TECHNIQUE • BEWARE •

Use your left leg to lift your opponent's left leg up, then wrap your leg over his left thigh.

Your right hand locks the opponent's right hand. Put your left leg over his shoulder to block the opponent's left arm. With your left tighten the grip on his collar and choke him.

Kimura while attacking the turtle guard

Kneel on the opponent's left side. Your right hand grabs his right forearm from the inside. Move around his head to the right side of your opponent.

The turtle position. The opponent defends himself by kneeling and resting on his elbows.

Your right hand keeps holding the opponent's right forearm and stretching his arm out. The opponent is forced to flip over.

Add your second hand to the grip. Lock the opponent's forearm. Stretch the arm and twist it up.

DANGEROUS TECHNIQUE • BEWARE •

BRAZILIAN JIU-JITSU

Choke from the top on all fours

Kneel on the opponent's right side. Your left hand blocks the opponent's right forearm, while your right hand grabs the left side of his gi collar.

2

The turtle position. The opponent defends himself by kneeling and resting on his elbows.

1

2

3

Take a firm grip of your opponent's gi collar. Climb onto his back and start shifting your body to the side until your opponent loses his balance.

7

4

5

6

DANGEROUS TECHNIQUE • BEWARE

Shift your body to the opponent's opposite (left) side. Roll onto your back. Your left hand blocks his left arm. Your right hand tightens the grip of the collar and chokes the opponent.

Attack from back mount using both collars and your shoulder on the back of your opponent's head

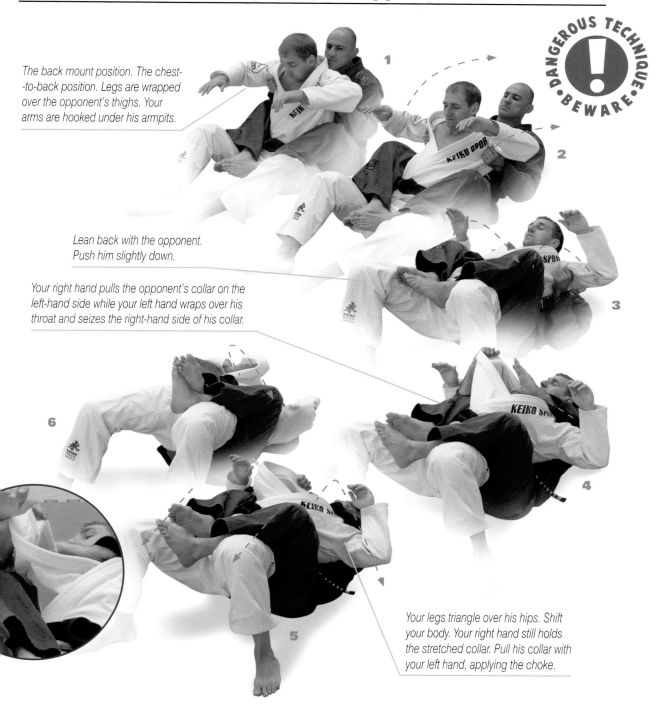

The back mount position. The chest--to-back position. Legs are wrapped over the opponent's thighs. Your arms are hooked under his armpits.

Lean back with the opponent. Push him slightly down.

Your right hand pulls the opponent's collar on the left-hand side while your left hand wraps over his throat and seizes the right-hand side of his collar.

Your legs triangle over his hips. Shift your body. Your right hand still holds the stretched collar. Pull his collar with your left hand, applying the choke.

DANGEROUS TECHNIQUE • BEWARE •

Back attack with one hand on the collar and one leg over the shoulder

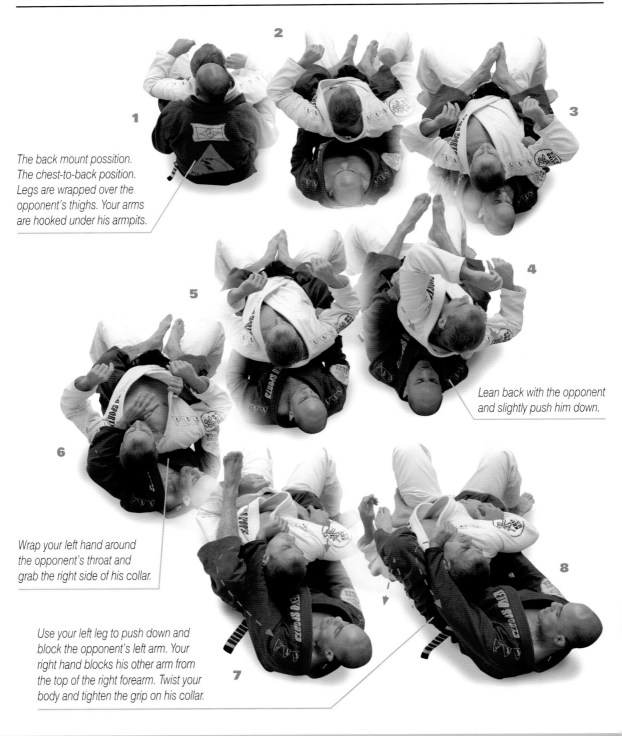

The back mount possition. The chest-to-back position. Legs are wrapped over the opponent's thighs. Your arms are hooked under his armpits.

Lean back with the opponent and slightly push him down.

Wrap your left hand around the opponent's throat and grab the right side of his collar.

Use your left leg to push down and block the opponent's left arm. Your right hand blocks his other arm from the top of the right forearm. Twist your body and tighten the grip on his collar.

(Different angle)

The back mount possition. The chest--to-back position. Legs are wrapped over the opponent's thighs. Your arms are hooked under his armpits.

Lean back with the opponent and slightly push him down. Wrap your left hand around the opponent's throat and grab the right side of his collar.

Use your left leg to push down and block the opponent's left arm. Your right hand blocks his other arm from the top of the right forearm. Twist your body and tighten the grip on his collar.

CHAPTER 9

Takedowns without Gi

Koshiki Taoshi - Ouchi Gari

Your right hand grabs the opponent's neck and pulls it towards you.

A strong pull makes him step forward. Your left hand blocks his right hand to prevent him from intercepting you.

Your right leg hooks the opponent's right leg from the inside. Grab his leg from underneath and take his balance.

Lift the opponent's right leg up, and enter with your hips.

The opponent falls backward. He is completely controlled and open to locks and other finishing techniques.

Cut the opponent's supporting leg out from the inside.

Oushi Gari - Kibisu Gaeshi

Strongly grab the back of your opponent's neck. Pull him towards you and put him off balance.

Pull the opponent towards you, step forward, and scoop his leg with your foot from the inside.

Enter, pivot, and kneel down. Your right hand pulls him down while your left leg continues blocking his back foot.

Block his front leg and grab the ankle of his back foot.

Assume the dominant position and finish the technique.

Kibisu Gaeshi

Grab your opponent's neck and pull him down. First block his front leg with your right foot, then grab the same leg with your left hand.

Pull up and straighten your opponent's left leg.

With your right foot cut out his supporting leg's ankle and pivot your body.

Sukui Nage

Strongly grab your opponent's neck. Control his right elbow with your left hand.

Dynamic movement: stand on your toes and shove his right hand up. Step forward and kneel down.

Underhook your opponent's left knee from the outside with your left hand.

Pivot and shift your weight down. The opponent falls backward. Assume the dominant position.

CHAPTER 10

The Closed Guard without Gi

BRAZILIAN JIU-JITSU

Arm bar from the closed guard

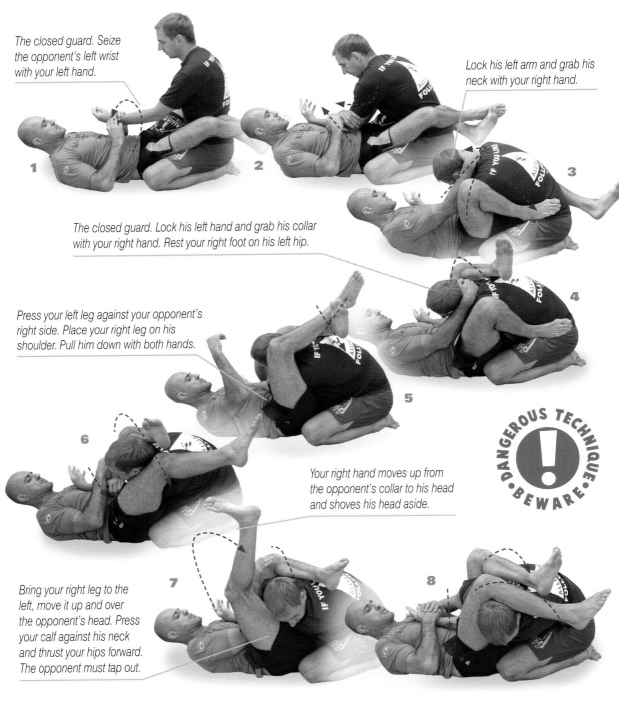

The closed guard. Seize the opponent's left wrist with your left hand.

Lock his left arm and grab his neck with your right hand.

The closed guard. Lock his left hand and grab his collar with your right hand. Rest your right foot on his left hip.

Press your left leg against your opponent's right side. Place your right leg on his shoulder. Pull him down with both hands.

Your right hand moves up from the opponent's collar to his head and shoves his head aside.

DANGEROUS TECHNIQUE • BEWARE •

Bring your right leg to the left, move it up and over the opponent's head. Press your calf against his neck and thrust your hips forward. The opponent must tap out.

Double arm bar from the closed guard

The closed guard. Seize both of the opponent's wrists, placing them on your chest and locking them. Open the guard. Place your knees on the sides of his shoulders.

Rest your feet on the opponent's hips. Thrust your hips forward.

Shift your right leg up and rest it on the opponent's left shoulder.

Shift your left leg and rest it on the opponent's right shoulder. Cross your feet behind his head. Press both your calves against his neck and thrust your hips forward. Both his elbows are joint-locked.

BRAZILIAN JIU-JITSU

Closed guard sweep to the mount

Grab the opponent's left wrist with your left hand. Your right hand grabs his left arm by the elbow. Pull his arm down and aside.

Hold the opponent's right shoulder with your right arm, and pull it back.

Slip your left hand underneath the opponent's right knee. Keep holding the opponent's right shoulder with your right hand. Rotate your body to the right. Start rolling.

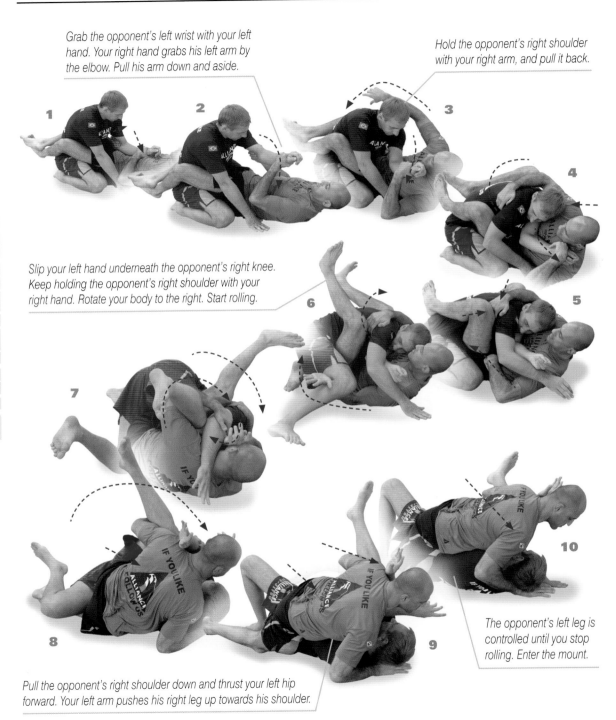

The opponent's left leg is controlled until you stop rolling. Enter the mount.

Pull the opponent's right shoulder down and thrust your left hip forward. Your left arm pushes his right leg up towards his shoulder.

Arm bar from the closed guard 2nd version

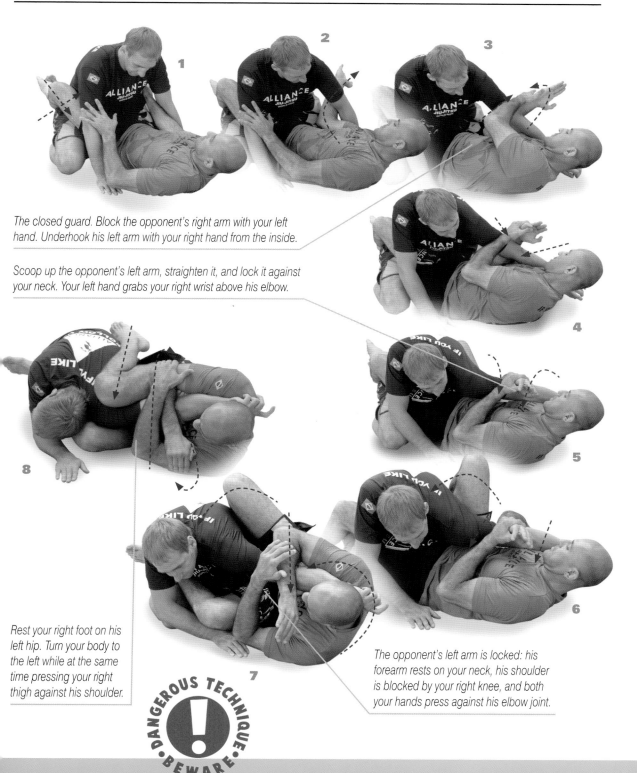

The closed guard. Block the opponent's right arm with your left hand. Underhook his left arm with your right hand from the inside.

Scoop up the opponent's left arm, straighten it, and lock it against your neck. Your left hand grabs your right wrist above his elbow.

Rest your right foot on his left hip. Turn your body to the left while at the same time pressing your right thigh against his shoulder.

The opponent's left arm is locked: his forearm rests on your neck, his shoulder is blocked by your right knee, and both your hands press against his elbow joint.

DANGEROUS TECHNIQUE · BEWARE ·

Wrist lock from the closed guard

DANGEROUS TECHNIQUE • BEWARE •

The closed guard. Seize the opponent's left wrist with your left hand.

Grab the opponent's left elbow with your right hand. Pull your opponent's arm down and aside.

Move your crossed legs (the closed guard) up the opponent's back. Place your right leg on the side of his left shoulder. Grab his left wrist with your right hand.

Double your grip on his left wrist. Apply a wrist lock to his left wrist with both your hands.

Kimura from the closed guard

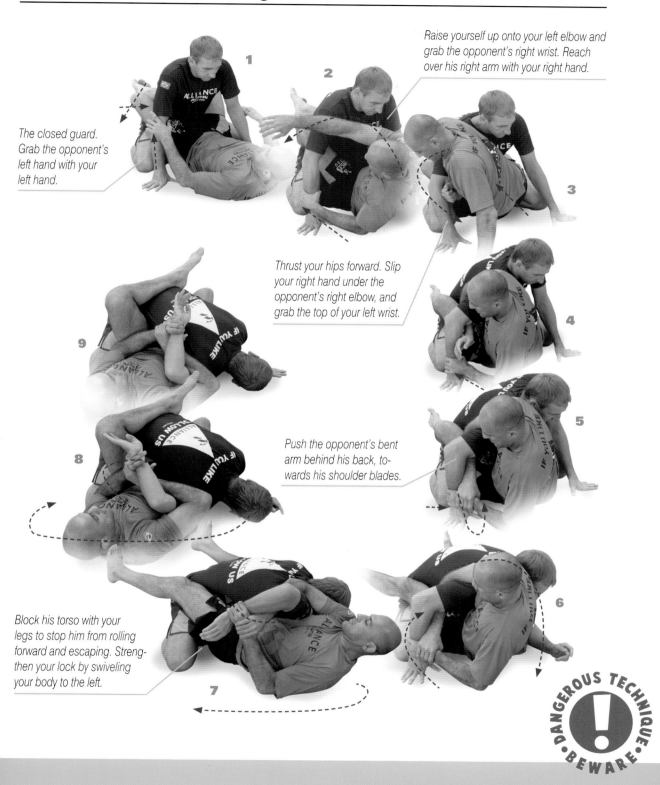

The closed guard.
Grab the opponent's
left hand with your
left hand.

Raise yourself up onto your left elbow and
grab the opponent's right wrist. Reach
over his right arm with your right hand.

Thrust your hips forward. Slip
your right hand under the
opponent's right elbow, and
grab the top of your left wrist.

Push the opponent's bent
arm behind his back, to-
wards his shoulder blades.

Block his torso with your
legs to stop him from rolling
forward and escaping. Strengthen your lock by swiveling
your body to the left.

DANGEROUS TECHNIQUE · BEWARE ·

Guillotine from the closed guard

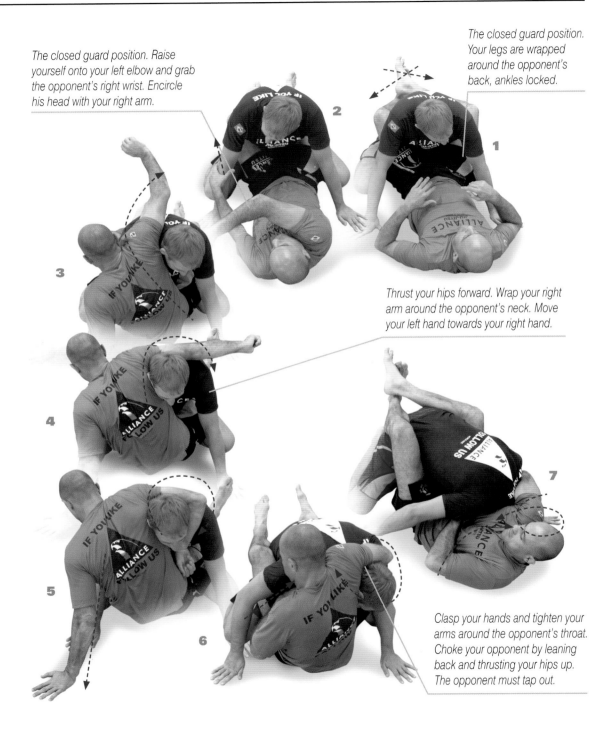

The closed guard position. Raise yourself onto your left elbow and grab the opponent's right wrist. Encircle his head with your right arm.

The closed guard position. Your legs are wrapped around the opponent's back, ankles locked.

Thrust your hips forward. Wrap your right arm around the opponent's neck. Move your left hand towards your right hand.

Clasp your hands and tighten your arms around the opponent's throat. Choke your opponent by leaning back and thrusting your hips up. The opponent must tap out.

(Different angle)

The closed guard position. Wrap your right arm around his head.

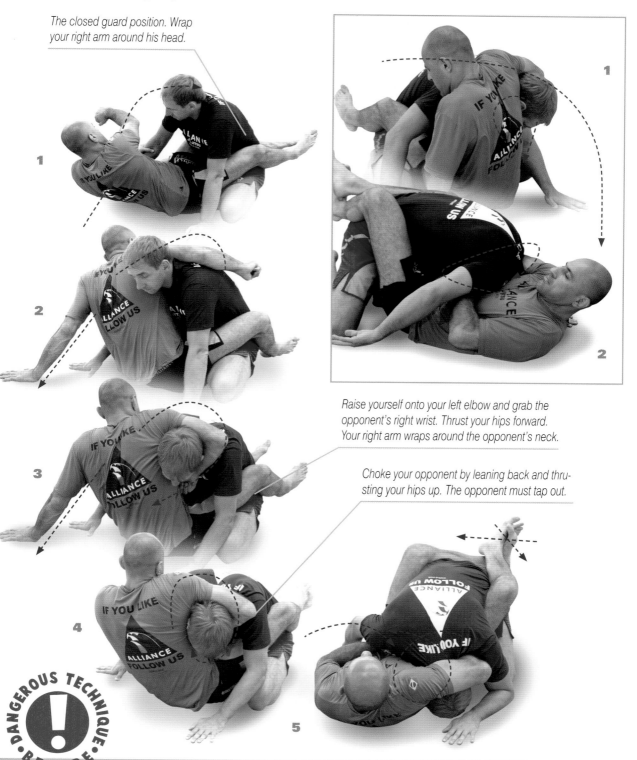

1

2

3

4

5

1

2

Raise yourself onto your left elbow and grab the opponent's right wrist. Thrust your hips forward. Your right arm wraps around the opponent's neck.

Choke your opponent by leaning back and thrusting your hips up. The opponent must tap out.

DANGEROUS TECHNIQUE · BEWARE ·

!

BRAZILIAN JIU-JITSU

"Hip bump" - Closed guard sweep to mount

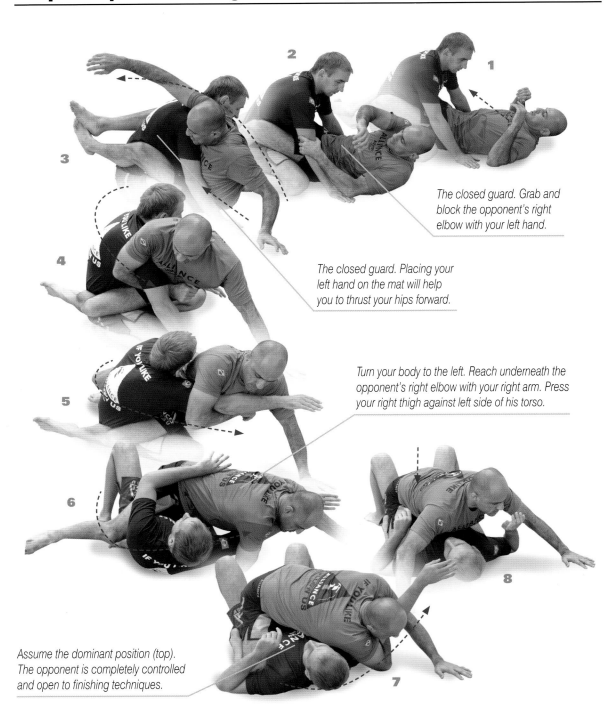

The closed guard. Grab and block the opponent's right elbow with your left hand.

The closed guard. Placing your left hand on the mat will help you to thrust your hips forward.

Turn your body to the left. Reach underneath the opponent's right elbow with your right arm. Press your right thigh against left side of his torso.

Assume the dominant position (top). The opponent is completely controlled and open to finishing techniques.

Arm bar from the closed guard 3rd version

The closed guard. Hold the opponent tightly in your arms. Use your arms to pull the opponent down and forward. Pass your arms over his head.

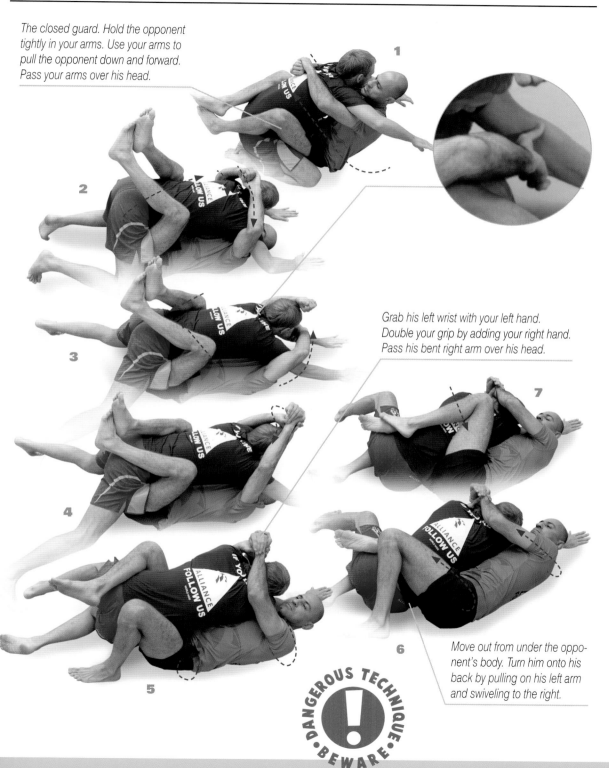

Grab his left wrist with your left hand. Double your grip by adding your right hand. Pass his bent right arm over his head.

Move out from under the opponent's body. Turn him onto his back by pulling on his left arm and swiveling to the right.

DANGEROUS TECHNIQUE · BEWARE ·

BRAZILIAN JIU-JITSU

Arm bar from the closed guard when your opponents stands

1

2

The opponent stands up, attempting to escape from the closed guard. Move your crossed legs up his back, towards his shoulder blades.

3

Swivel to the left. Block his left leg from the inside with your right hand. Your left hand secures his right hand.

Move your left leg over the opponent's head. Thrust your hips forward and press your calf against his neck.

Move your left leg over his head. Thrust your hips forward. Press your calf against his neck.

4

5

6

(Different angle)

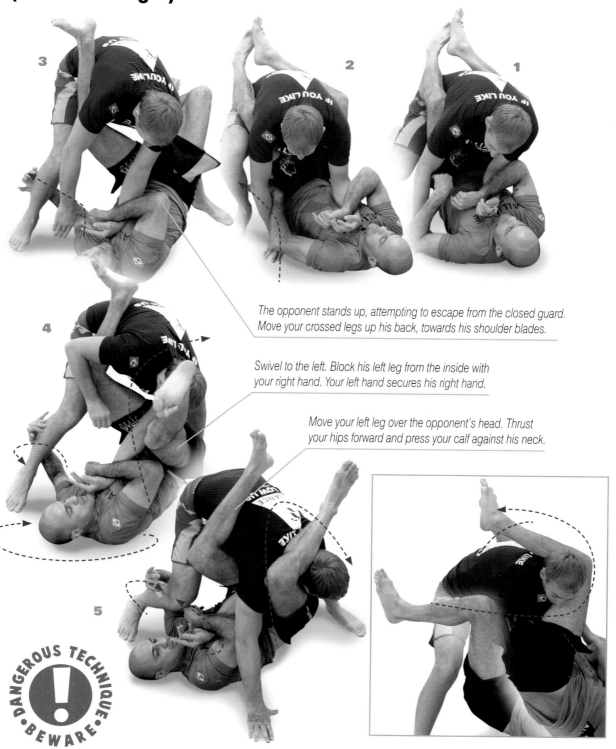

3

2

1

The opponent stands up, attempting to escape from the closed guard. Move your crossed legs up his back, towards his shoulder blades.

Swivel to the left. Block his left leg from the inside with your right hand. Your left hand secures his right hand.

Move your left leg over the opponent's head. Thrust your hips forward and press your calf against his neck.

4

5

DANGEROUS TECHNIQUE ∙BEWARE∙ !

CHAPTER 11

Passing the Closed Guard without Gi

BRAZILIAN JIU-JITSU

Standing closed guard pass

Your opponent is in the closed guard position. Seize his throat with your right hand. Your left hand grabs his pants on his left hip.

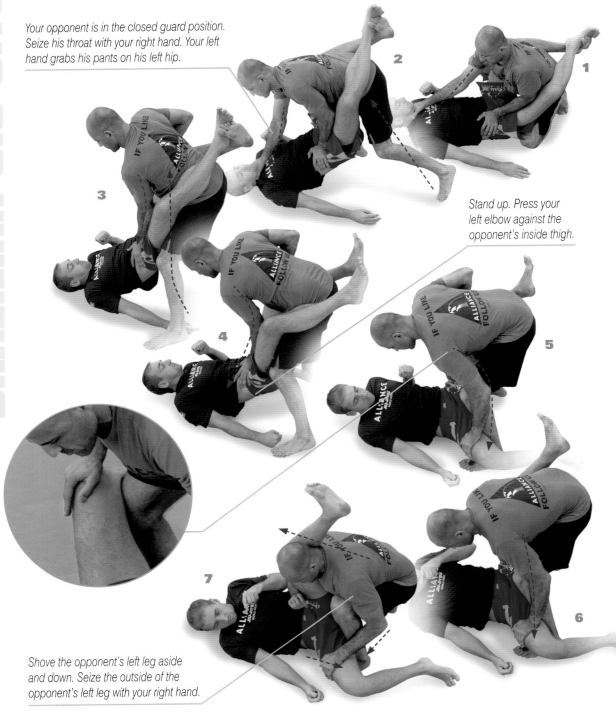

Stand up. Press your left elbow against the opponent's inside thigh.

Shove the opponent's left leg aside and down. Seize the outside of the opponent's left leg with your right hand.

Press your right shoulder against the opponent's thigh. Clasp your hands together and press your entire body weight against him.

Press your right shoulder against the opponent's thigh. Seize his pants with your left hand.

Forcefully push your opponent onto his side. Your left hand supports the move. Roll him onto his back.

Forcefully push your opponent onto his side. Your left hand supports the move. Rolling the opponent. The opponent is controlled in the side position.

BRAZILIAN JIU-JITSU

Closed guard pass while holding your opponent's wrist

The opponent is in the closed guard position. Seize his right arm with your left hand, extend the arm, and pin the arm against the mat.

Stand and grip the mat with your toes while straightening your legs. Lower your chest and thrust your body forward. Lift your hips up. The opponent keeps the closed guard position.

Your left hand moves the opponent's right arm along the mat. Pass the grip of his right arm to your right hand.

Lower your hips. Your right hand locks the opponent's right arm under his body. Draw your hips back.

8

Use your left arm to lift and push yourself away. Slide your body down his body.

9

10

Spread the opponent's legs by pushing his right knee to the outside with your left hand. Open the guard. Escape from the guard with your left leg, then pull your right knee out. His right arm locks under his own body.

11

Shift to the side position. Your left arm moves underneath his neck. Let go of his right arm.

12

13

14

BRAZILIAN JIU-JITSU

Closed guard pass while holding your opponent's wrist

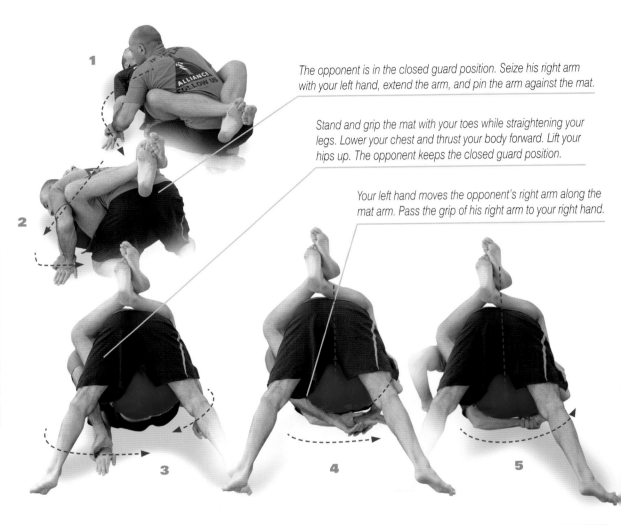

The opponent is in the closed guard position. Seize his right arm with your left hand, extend the arm, and pin the arm against the mat.

Stand and grip the mat with your toes while straightening your legs. Lower your chest and thrust your body forward. Lift your hips up. The opponent keeps the closed guard position.

Your left hand moves the opponent's right arm along the mat arm. Pass the grip of his right arm to your right hand.

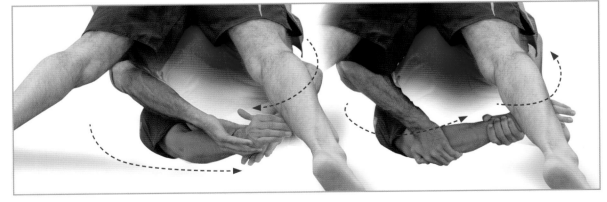

Your right hand locks the opponent's right arm under his body. Draw your hips back.

Use your left arm to lift and push yourself away. Lower your hips and slide your body down.

Open the guard with your left arm by shoving his knee down. Escape from the guard by removing your left leg, then pulling your right knee out. His right arm locks under his own body.

Shift to the side position. Your left arm moves underneath his neck. Release his right arm.

Standing closed guard pass controlling your opponent's arm

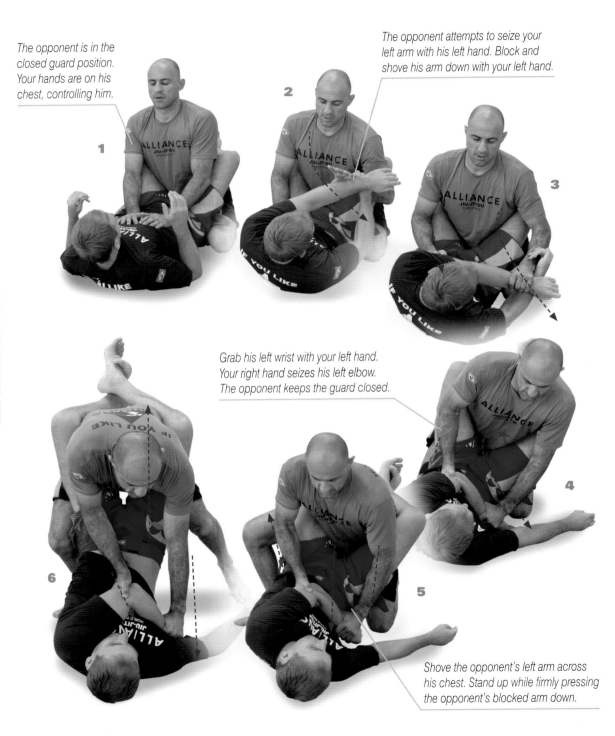

The opponent is in the closed guard position. Your hands are on his chest, controlling him.

The opponent attempts to seize your left arm with his left hand. Block and shove his arm down with your left hand.

Grab his left wrist with your left hand. Your right hand seizes his left elbow. The opponent keeps the guard closed.

Shove the opponent's left arm across his chest. Stand up while firmly pressing the opponent's blocked arm down.

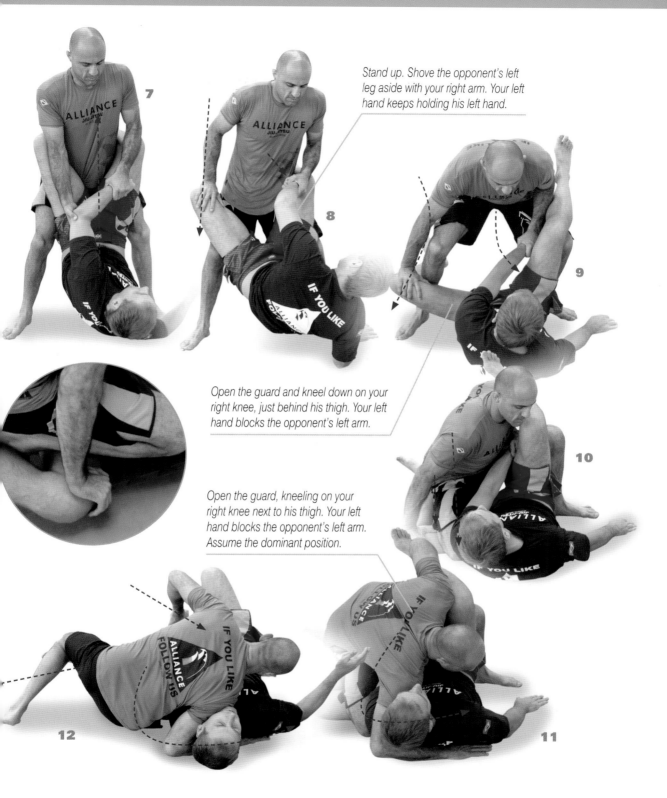

7

8

Stand up. Shove the opponent's left leg aside with your right arm. Your left hand keeps holding his left hand.

9

Open the guard and kneel down on your right knee, just behind his thigh. Your left hand blocks the opponent's left arm.

10

Open the guard, kneeling on your right knee next to his thigh. Your left hand blocks the opponent's left arm. Assume the dominant position.

12

11

CHAPTER 12

Butterfly Guard without Gi

"Over-under" Butterfly guard sweep

The butterfly guard position. Your right arm hooks under the opponent's left arm. Your right hand presses his back. Your right foot is underneath his left thigh.

Simultaneous movement: force his left thigh up with your right foot while dynamically turning your body to the left. Your left hand pulls him down and to the left while your right hand pushes him up and to the left.

Your right hand holds the opponent's left arm to prevent him from placing his hand on the mat, thus stopping the rolling movement. Your head is next to his head.

12

11

10

The opponent is on his back. Brace your left leg on the mat and push your body up. Push the opponent's right hand up. Place your head on the mat next to his head to block his sideway movements.

Slide your knee against his belly, then enter the mount. The dominant position (top). The opponent is open to locks and finishing techniques.

9

8

7

Butterfly guard sweep from back attack

The butterfly position. The opponent attacks your hips. Seize his right shoulder with your left hand. Your right hand blocks his left shoulder.

Lean back. Underhook his right leg from the inside, then cross your ankles

Rest your right hand on the mat. Push your body up. Reach under his left armpit with your left arm.

Lean back. Hook your right leg underneath his left knee. Lower your body to the mat. Your left hand pulls him back while your right leg forces him up.

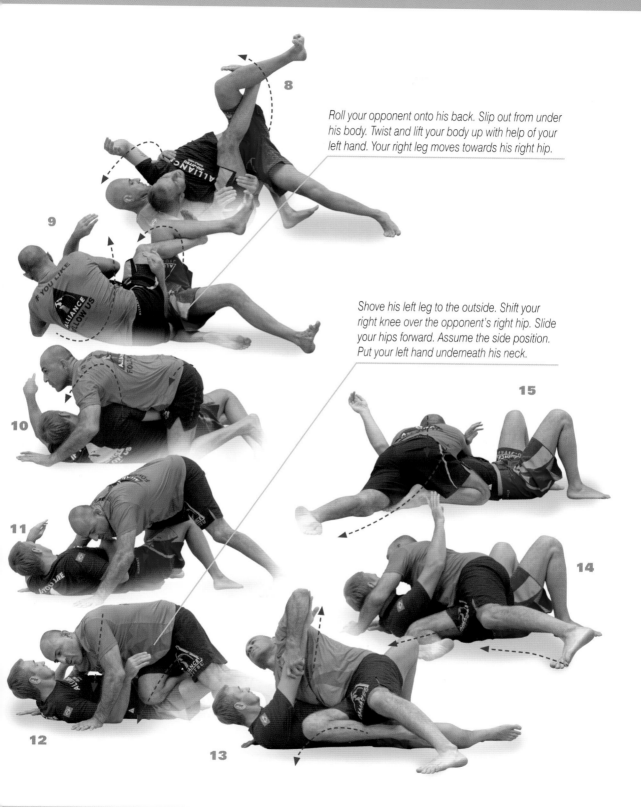

8

Roll your opponent onto his back. Slip out from under his body. Twist and lift your body up with help of your left hand. Your right leg moves towards his right hip.

9

Shove his left leg to the outside. Shift your right knee over the opponent's right hip. Slide your hips forward. Assume the side position. Put your left hand underneath his neck.

15

10

11

14

12

13

Butterfly Guard without Gi   **127**

Butterfly guard sweep to knee cut across

The butterfly position. The opponent attacks your hips. Seize his right shoulder with your left hand. Your right hand blocks his left shoulder.

Lean back. Underhook his right leg from the inside, then cross your ankles.

Rest your right hand on the mat. Push your body up. Reach under his left armpit with your left arm.

Lean back. Hook your right leg underneath his left knee. Lower your body to the mat. Your left hand pulls him back while your right leg forces him up.

Slide your hips forward. Assume the side position. Put your left hand underneath his neck.

15

14

13

16

12

Roll your opponent onto his back. Slip out from under his body. Twist and lift your body up with help of your left hand. Your right leg moves towards his right hip. Shove his left leg outside. Shift your right knee over the opponent's right hip.

11

9

10

CHAPTER 13

Passing the Open guard without Gi

Knee cut across open guard pass

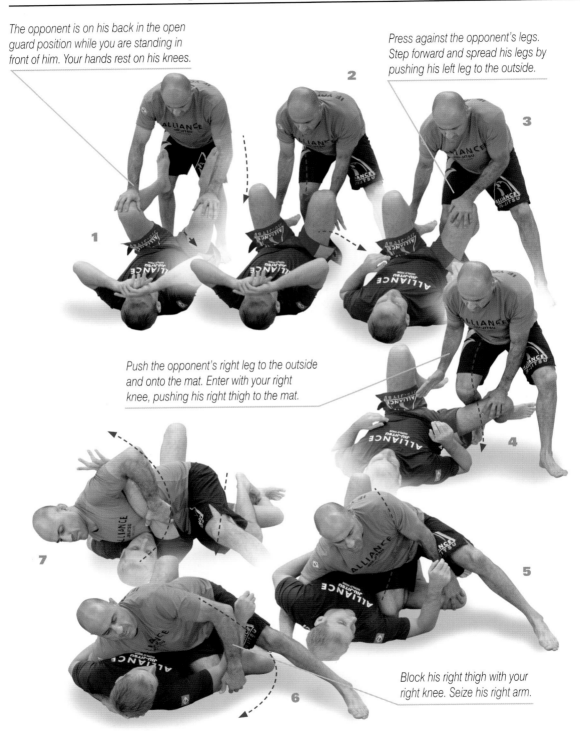

The opponent is on his back in the open guard position while you are standing in front of him. Your hands rest on his knees.

Press against the opponent's legs. Step forward and spread his legs by pushing his left leg to the outside.

Push the opponent's right leg to the outside and onto the mat. Enter with your right knee, pushing his right thigh to the mat.

Block his right thigh with your right knee. Seize his right arm.

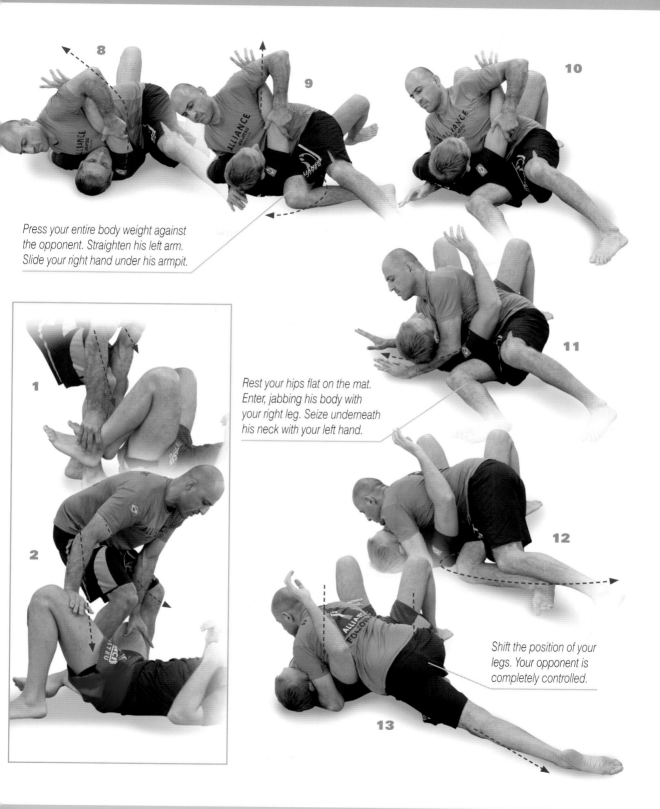

Press your entire body weight against the opponent. Straighten his left arm. Slide your right hand under his armpit.

Rest your hips flat on the mat. Enter, jabbing his body with your right leg. Seize underneath his neck with your left hand.

Shift the position of your legs. Your opponent is completely controlled.

Knee cut across open guard pass when the opponent blocks with his leg

The opponent is on his back in open guard position while you are standing in front of him. Your hands rest on his knees. Spread his legs by pushing his right leg to the outside and step forward. Enter with your right knee.

Block the opponent's right thigh with your right knee. Shove his left leg to the right with your right arm.

Grab his right wrist with your left hand.

Hook your right arm under the opponent's right knee.

Switch your grip on the opponent's right wrist to your right hand.

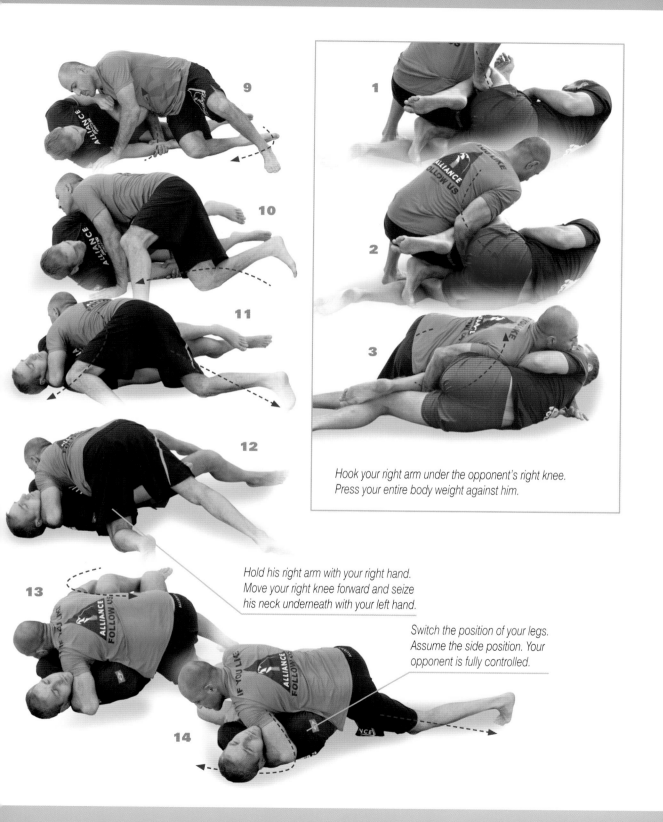

Hook your right arm under the opponent's right knee.
Press your entire body weight against him.

Hold his right arm with your right hand.
Move your right knee forward and seize
his neck underneath with your left hand.

Switch the position of your legs.
Assume the side position. Your
opponent is fully controlled.

Knee cut across open guard pass when the opponent blocks with his leg

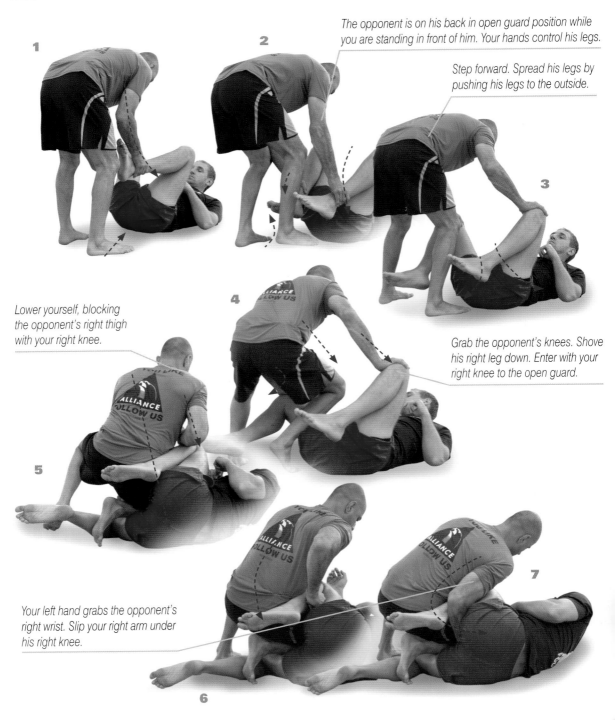

The opponent is on his back in open guard position while you are standing in front of him. Your hands control his legs.

Step forward. Spread his legs by pushing his legs to the outside.

Lower yourself, blocking the opponent's right thigh with your right knee.

Grab the opponent's knees. Shove his right leg down. Enter with your right knee to the open guard.

Your left hand grabs the opponent's right wrist. Slip your right arm under his right knee.

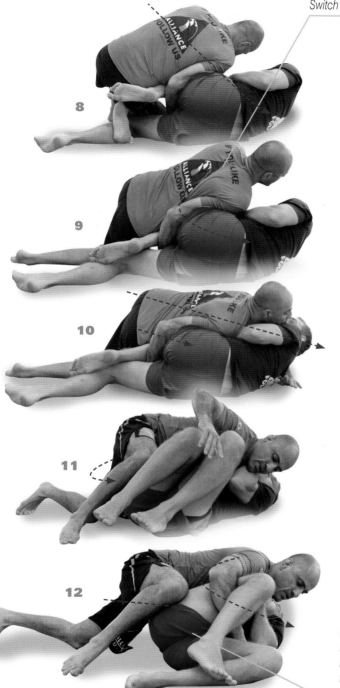

Move your right arm under the opponent's right knee. Switch your grip on his right arm to your right hand.

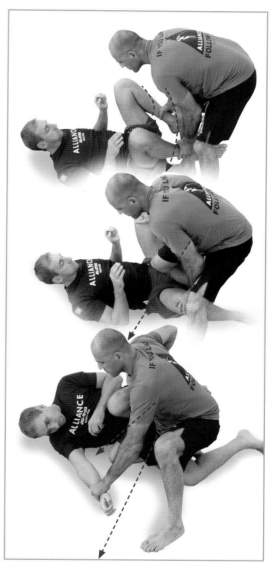

Hold the opponent's right arm with your right hand. Move your right knee forward and grab his neck from underneath with your left hand. Shift the position of your legs. Assume the side control position. Your opponent is completely controlled.

Passing the Open guard without Gi   **137**

Knee cut across to high leg back

The opponent is on his back in the open guard position while you are standing in front of him. Your hands control his legs. Step forward. Spread the opponent's legs by pushing his left leg to the left.

Grab the opponent's knees. Shove his right leg down. Enter the opponent's open guard with your right knee. Lower yourself, blocking his right thigh with your right knee.

The opponent shifts to the half guard position. He locks his legs around your right leg.

Move your hips and your left leg behind the opponent, so that you end up behind his back.

BRAZILIAN JIU-JITSU

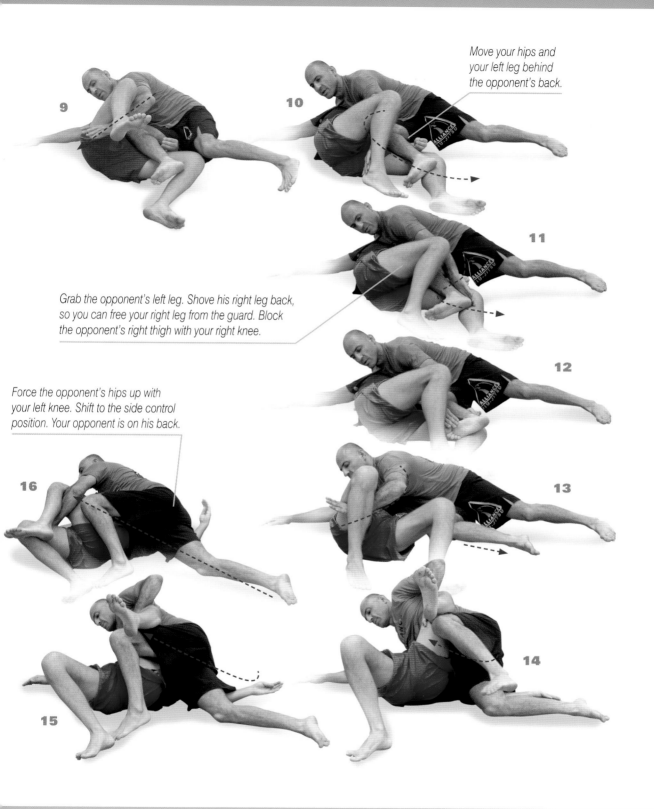

Move your hips and your left leg behind the opponent's back.

Grab the opponent's left leg. Shove his right leg back, so you can free your right leg from the guard. Block the opponent's right thigh with your right knee.

Force the opponent's hips up with your left knee. Shift to the side control position. Your opponent is on his back.

BRAZILIAN JIU-JITSU

Knee cut across to high leg back

The opponent is on his back in the open guard position while you are standing in front of him. Your hands control his legs.

Step forward. Spread the opponent's legs by pushing his left leg to the left. Push his right leg outside.

Enter the opponent's open guard with your right knee. Lower yourself, blocking the opponent's right thigh with your right knee. Move your hips and your left leg over the opponent's hips and behind his back.

The opponent shifts to half guard position. He wraps his legs around your right leg.

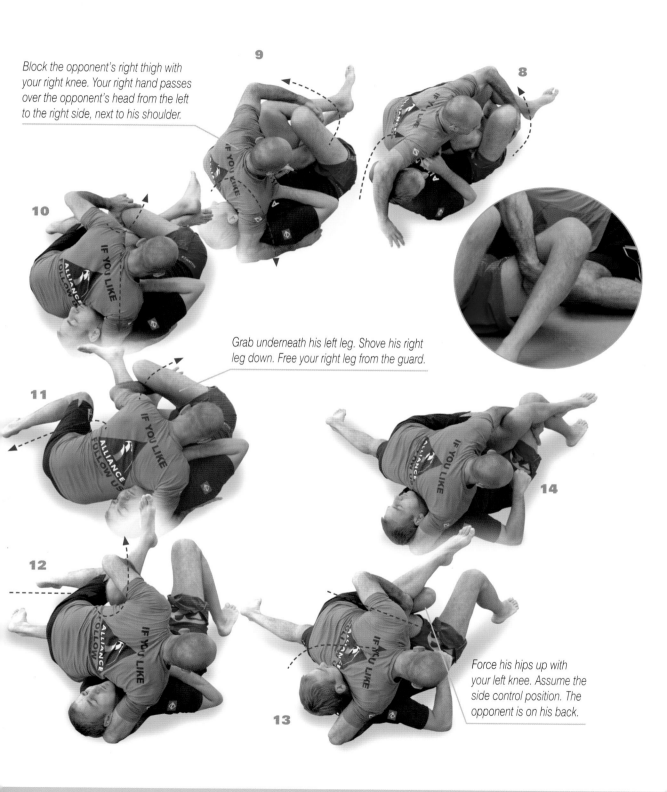

Block the opponent's right thigh with your right knee. Your right hand passes over the opponent's head from the left to the right side, next to his shoulder.

Grab underneath his left leg. Shove his right leg down. Free your right leg from the guard.

Force his hips up with your left knee. Assume the side control position. The opponent is on his back.

Knee cut across to side control

The opponent keeps a closed guard. Grab his right wrist with your left hand. Seize his lapel with your right hand.

Shift your grip on his right arm behind his back to your right hand.

Slide your left leg out from the guard. Move your hips forward. Pull your right leg out from the guard.

(Different angle)

1

The opponent is in the closed guard position. Grab the opponent's right wrist with your left hand.

2

3

Slide your left leg from the guard. Move your hips forward. Pull your right leg out from the guard.

5

4

6

8

7

Shove the opponent's right leg down to the mat with your left hand. Your right hand holds his right arm behind his back.

Shove the opponent's right leg down to the mat with your left hand. Your right hand holds his right arm behind his back.

Knee cut across to the mount

Grab the opponent's knees. Spread his legs by pushing his left leg to the outside.

Push the opponent's left leg to the outside. Enter with your knee. Block his right thigh with your right shin. Grab his right arm.

Press your body weight against him and straighten his left arm. The opponent wraps his legs over your right leg — the half guard position.

Pin his right arm to the mat.

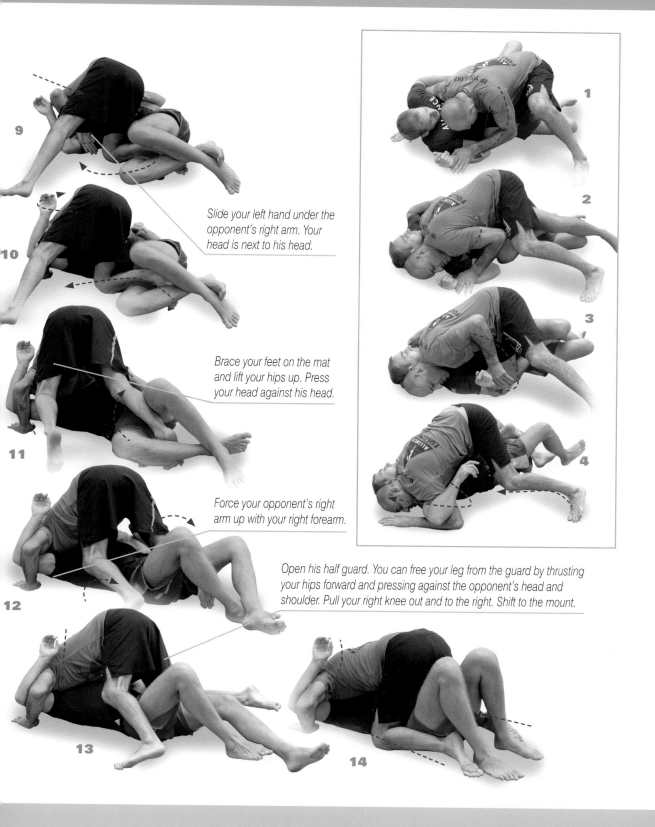

Slide your left hand under the opponent's right arm. Your head is next to his head.

Brace your feet on the mat and lift your hips up. Press your head against his head.

Force your opponent's right arm up with your right forearm.

Open his half guard. You can free your leg from the guard by thrusting your hips forward and pressing against the opponent's head and shoulder. Pull your right knee out and to the right. Shift to the mount.

CHAPTER 14

Side Control without Gi

BRAZILIAN JIU-JITSU

Same side arm bar from side control

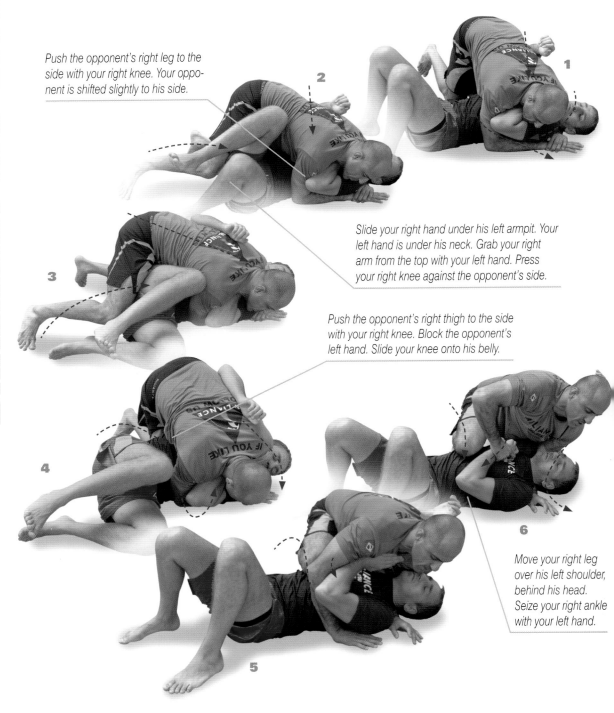

Push the opponent's right leg to the side with your right knee. Your opponent is shifted slightly to his side.

Slide your right hand under his left armpit. Your left hand is under his neck. Grab your right arm from the top with your left hand. Press your right knee against the opponent's side.

Push the opponent's right thigh to the side with your right knee. Block the opponent's left hand. Slide your knee onto his belly.

Move your right leg over his left shoulder, behind his head. Seize your right ankle with your left hand.

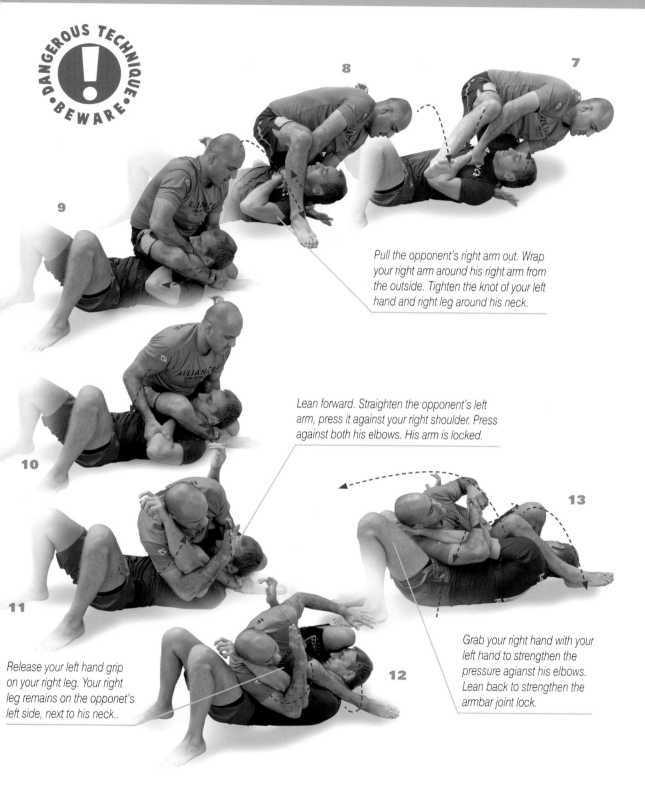

7

Pull the opponent's right arm out. Wrap your right arm around his right arm from the outside. Tighten the knot of your left hand and right leg around his neck.

8

9

Lean forward. Straighten the opponent's left arm, press it against your right shoulder. Press against both his elbows. His arm is locked.

10

11

Release your left hand grip on your right leg. Your right leg remains on the opponet's left side, next to his neck..

12

13

Grab your right hand with your left hand to strengthen the pressure agianst his elbows. Lean back to strengthen the armbar joint lock.

Same side arm bar from side control off triangle attack

The dominant side position. Place your left arm underneath the opponent's neck. Your right hand is tucked under his left arm. Clasp your hands.

Shove the opponent's right thigh to the left side with your right knee. Your opponent is shifted slightly to his side.

While the opponent is lying on his back, pin him to the ground. Your left hand is under his neck. Block his left arm with your right arm. Slide your knee onto his belly.

Shift your right leg over the opponent's shoulder. Grab your right leg with your left hand. Wedge his neck and head between your right leg and your left arm.

Wrap your right arm around his left elbow.

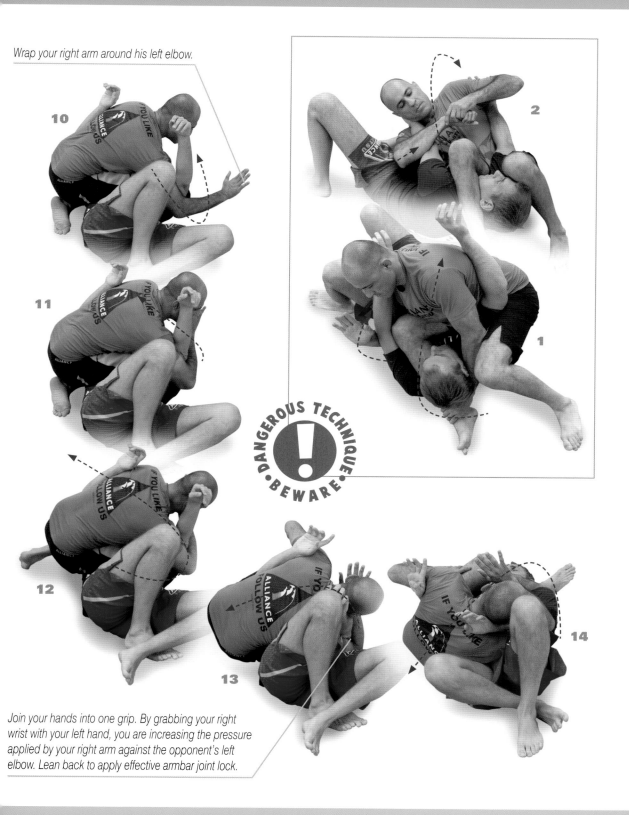

10

11

12

13

14

1

2

DANGEROUS TECHNIQUE • BEWARE •

Join your hands into one grip. By grabbing your right wrist with your left hand, you are increasing the pressure applied by your right arm against the opponent's left elbow. Lean back to apply effective armbar joint lock.

Same side arm bar from side control off triangle attack

Wrap your right hand around the opponent's left elbow from the outside.

Shove the opponent's right thigh to the side with your right knee. Your opponent is shifted slightly to his side. Block his left arm with your right arm. Slide your knee onto his belly.

Shift your left leg over his shoulder. Grab your right ankle with your left hand. Wedge his head between your right leg and your left forearm.

Join your hands into one grip. Grab your right wrist with your left hand. By grabbing your right arm with your left hand you are increasing the pressure applied by your right arm against the opponent's left elbow. Lean back to apply effective armbar joint lock.

DANGEROUS TECHNIQUE · BEWARE

Mount sliding knee to belly

The dominant side position. Your left arm is under the opponent's neck. Your right hand is tucked under his left arm. Join your hands into one grip.

Shove the opponent's right thigh to the side with your right knee. Your opponent is shifted slightly to his side.

Move your body forward. Squeeze the opponent tightly with your arms. Slide your knee onto his right hip. Press your biceps against the opponent's arm.

Open the opponent's position by thrusting your hips forward and pressing your right arm against his left arm. Shift your leg to the outside and enter the mount.

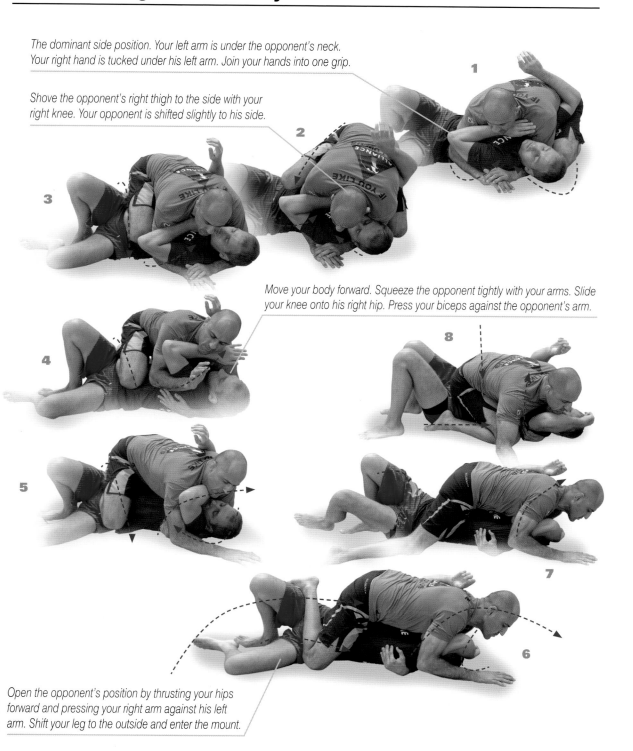

Mount sliding knee to belly

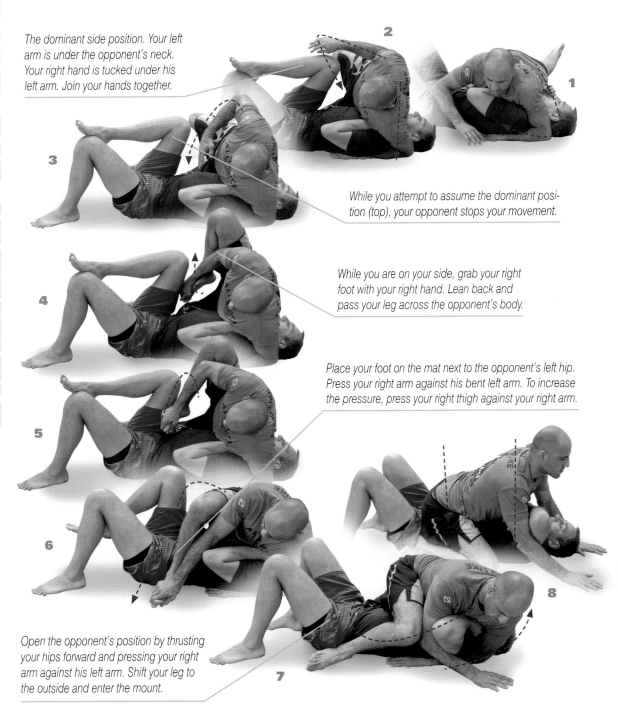

The dominant side position. Your left arm is under the opponent's neck. Your right hand is tucked under his left arm. Join your hands together.

While you attempt to assume the dominant position (top), your opponent stops your movement.

While you are on your side, grab your right foot with your right hand. Lean back and pass your leg across the opponent's body.

Place your foot on the mat next to the opponent's left hip. Press your right arm against his bent left arm. To increase the pressure, press your right thigh against your right arm.

Open the opponent's position by thrusting your hips forward and pressing your right arm against his left arm. Shift your leg to the outside and enter the mount.

Mount to arm triangle

The dominant side position. Your left arm is under the opponent's neck. Your right hand is tucked under his left arm. Push his left elbow and arm up and to the right.

Shove the opponent's right thigh to the side with your right knee. The opponent is just off his back. Force your head under his left arm.

Push your right hand against the opponent's right knee. Put your knee on his hip. Press your head against his arm.

Pass your right leg over your opponent. Planting your right leg on the mat will help you to forcefully press your head against the opponent's arm.

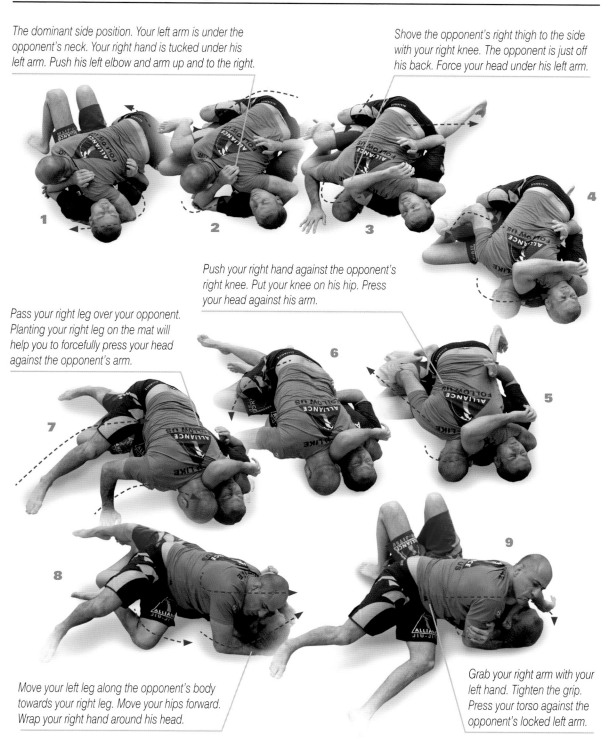

Move your left leg along the opponent's body towards your right leg. Move your hips forward. Wrap your right hand around his head.

Grab your right arm with your left hand. Tighten the grip. Press your torso against the opponent's locked left arm.

BRAZILIAN JIU-JITSU

Kimura from the north-south position

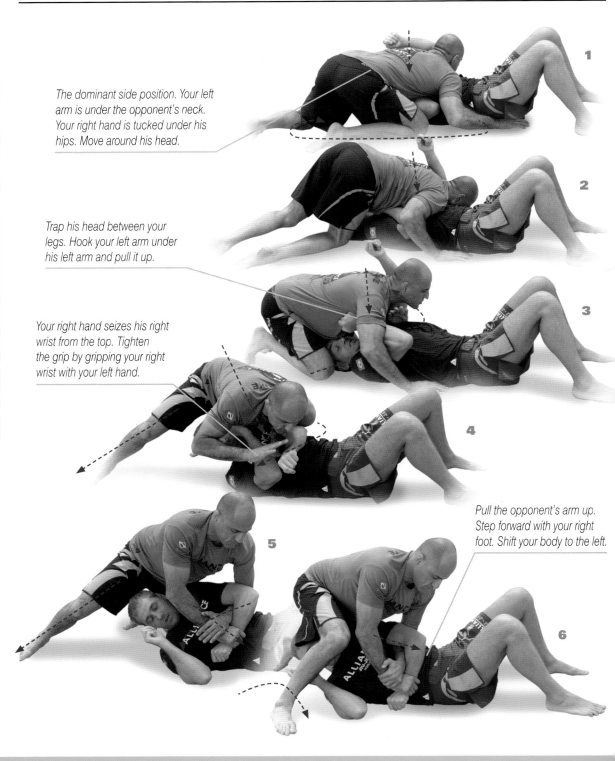

The dominant side position. Your left arm is under the opponent's neck. Your right hand is tucked under his hips. Move around his head.

Trap his head between your legs. Hook your left arm under his left arm and pull it up.

Your right hand seizes his right wrist from the top. Tighten the grip by gripping your right wrist with your left hand.

Pull the opponent's arm up. Step forward with your right foot. Shift your body to the left.

Kneel on your right knee to block the opponent's right arm. Plant your left foot on the mat next to his side.

7

Straighten your body. You have the opponent's left arm controlled — pull it up.

8

1

2

3

4

9

10

DANGEROUS TECHNIQUE • BEWARE •

Turn to the left, forcing his left arm behind his back. Tighten the lock by moving his bent arm towards his shoulder blades

BRAZILIAN JIU-JITSU

Opposite side arm bar from side control

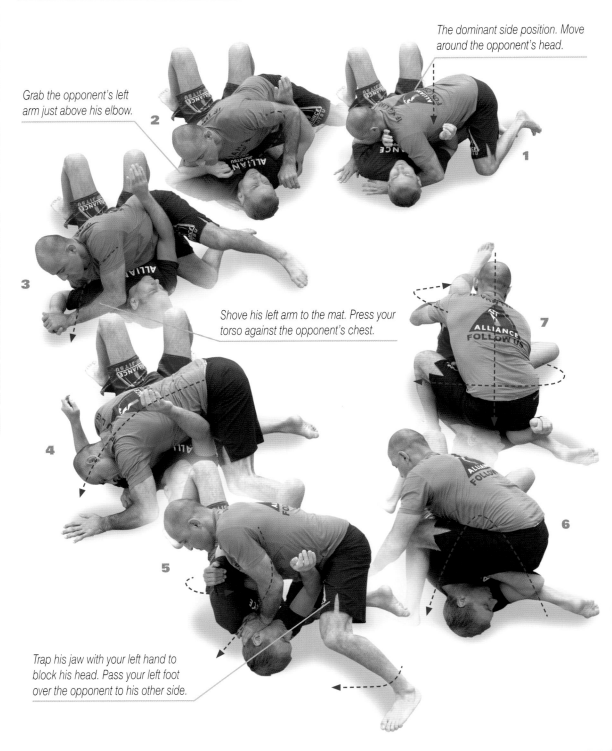

The dominant side position. Move around the opponent's head.

Grab the opponent's left arm just above his elbow.

Shove his left arm to the mat. Press your torso against the opponent's chest.

Trap his jaw with your left hand to block his head. Pass your left foot over the opponent to his other side.

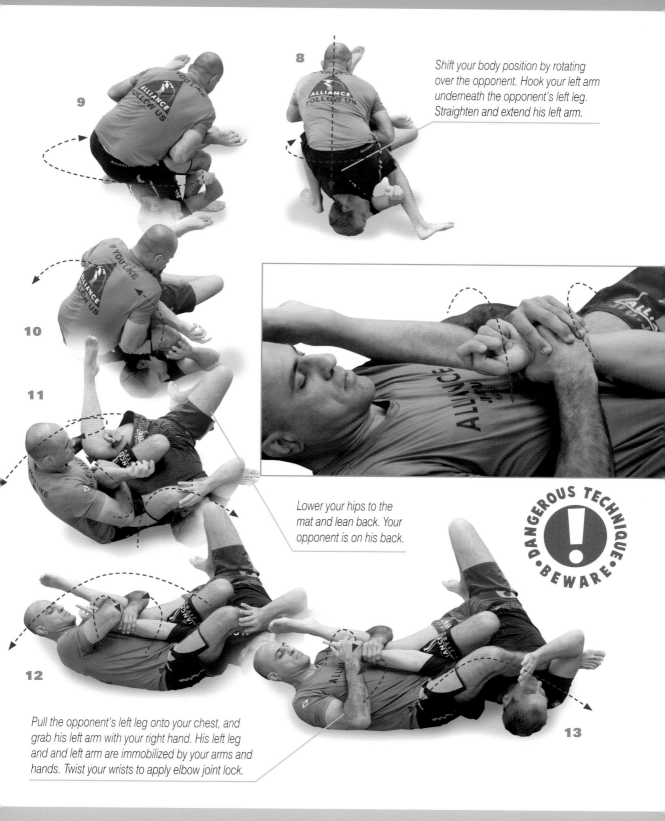

8 Shift your body position by rotating over the opponent. Hook your left arm underneath the opponent's left leg. Straighten and extend his left arm.

9

10

11

Lower your hips to the mat and lean back. Your opponent is on his back.

DANGEROUS TECHNIQUE · BEWARE ·

12

Pull the opponent's left leg onto your chest, and grab his left arm with your right hand. His left leg and and left arm are immobilized by your arms and hands. Twist your wrists to apply elbow joint lock.

13

BRAZILIAN JIU-JITSU

Arm bar from north-south Kimura

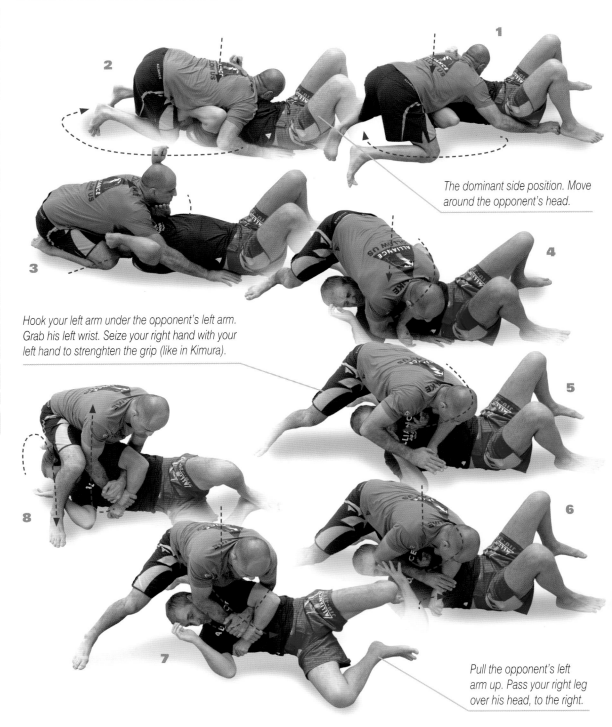

The dominant side position. Move around the opponent's head.

Hook your left arm under the opponent's left arm. Grab his left wrist. Seize your right hand with your left hand to strenghten the grip (like in Kimura).

Pull the opponent's left arm up. Pass your right leg over his head, to the right.

The opponent's arm is in a keylock. Lower your hips on the mat. Lean back.

10

11

9

Lean back. Put your left leg across his chest. Straighten and extend his left arm.

12

15

13

14

Squeeze your knees together. Twist his left arm so that his thumb points up. Extend his arm to apply an elbow joint lock.

DANGEROUS TECHNIQUE · BEWARE ·

CHAPTER 15

The Mount without Gi

Arm bar from the mount

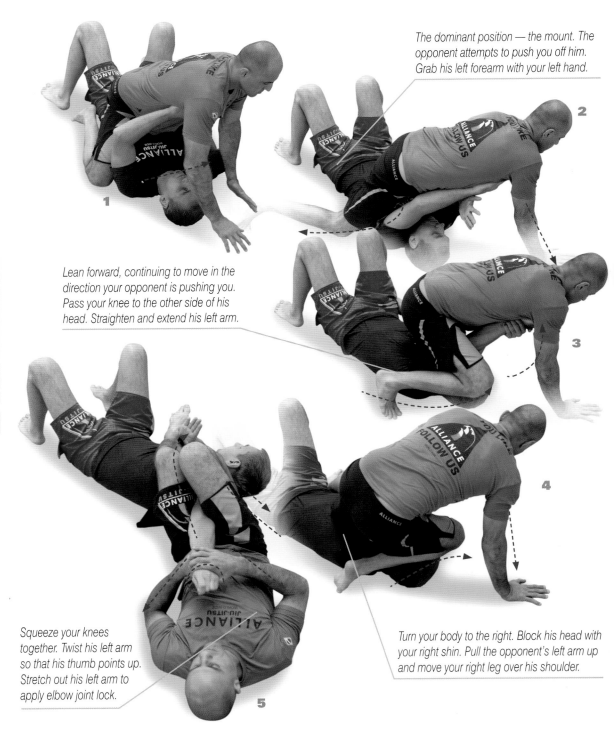

The dominant position — the mount. The opponent attempts to push you off him. Grab his left forearm with your left hand.

Lean forward, continuing to move in the direction your opponent is pushing you. Pass your knee to the other side of his head. Straighten and extend his left arm.

Turn your body to the right. Block his head with your right shin. Pull the opponent's left arm up and move your right leg over his shoulder.

Squeeze your knees together. Twist his left arm so that his thumb points up. Stretch out his left arm to apply elbow joint lock.

(Different angle)

The dominant position — the mount. The opponent attempts to push you off him. Grab his left forearm with your left hand.

Lean forward, continuing to move in the direction your opponent is pushing you. Pass your knee to the other side of his head. Straighten and extend his left arm.

Slide your body to the side. Lean back. Pull up and straighten his left arm and move your right.

Squeeze your knees together. Twist his left arm so that his thumb points up. Stretch out his left arm to apply elbow joint lock.

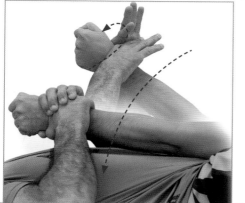

DANGEROUS TECHNIQUE · BEWARE ·

Arm bar from the mounted arm triangle

The dominant position — the mount. Lean forward. Move your right knee foward and close to the opponent's left shoulder. Move your left leg over his right shoulder.

Lean your body to the right. Hook your left arm under the opponent's left arm.

Seize your right arm from the top with your left hand. The opponent's neck and left arm are trapped between your arms.

Slide your right arm under the opponent's neck and pull his head up. Move your left foot over the opponent's body and rest it under his right armpit.

Grab the opponent's left wrist from the top. Seize your right forearm with your left hand. The opponent's head and left arm are closed in a keylock.

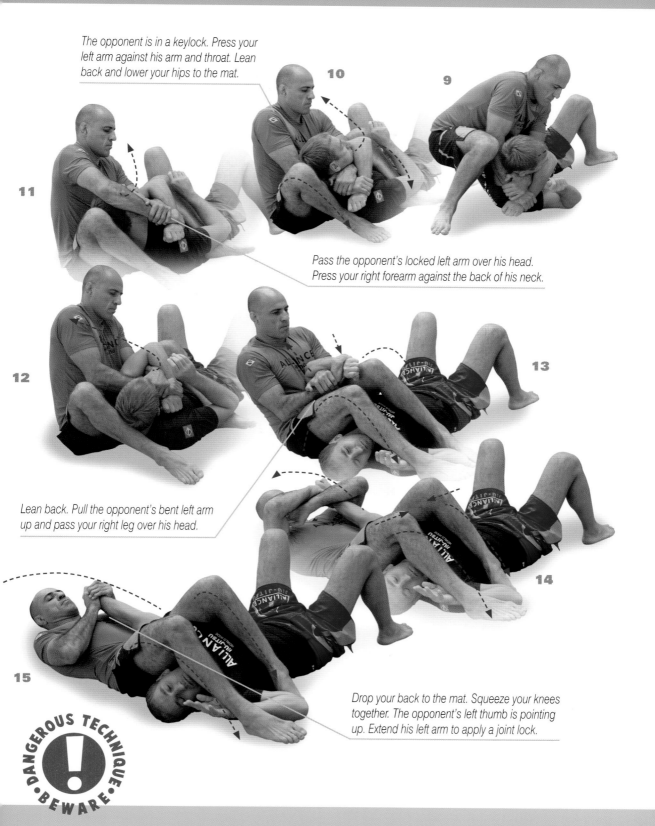

The opponent is in a keylock. Press your left arm against his arm and throat. Lean back and lower your hips to the mat.

Pass the opponent's locked left arm over his head. Press your right forearm against the back of his neck.

Lean back. Pull the opponent's bent left arm up and pass your right leg over his head.

Drop your back to the mat. Squeeze your knees together. The opponent's left thumb is pointing up. Extend his left arm to apply a joint lock.

DANGEROUS TECHNIQUE · BEWARE ·

CHAPTER 16

Half Guard without Gi

BJJ

Deep half guard sweep dominating your opponent's leg

Keep the opponent in the half guard position. Seize his right thigh with your left hand.

Pull the opponent's right thigh up with your left hand. Push his right thigh up with your right leg. Turn your body to the left and slide under the opponent's hips.

Hook underneath the opponent's right thigh with your right arm and grip it with your biceps.

Grab his right wrist with your left hand and pass it to your right hand. His right leg and right arm are locked between your legs and a hand grip.

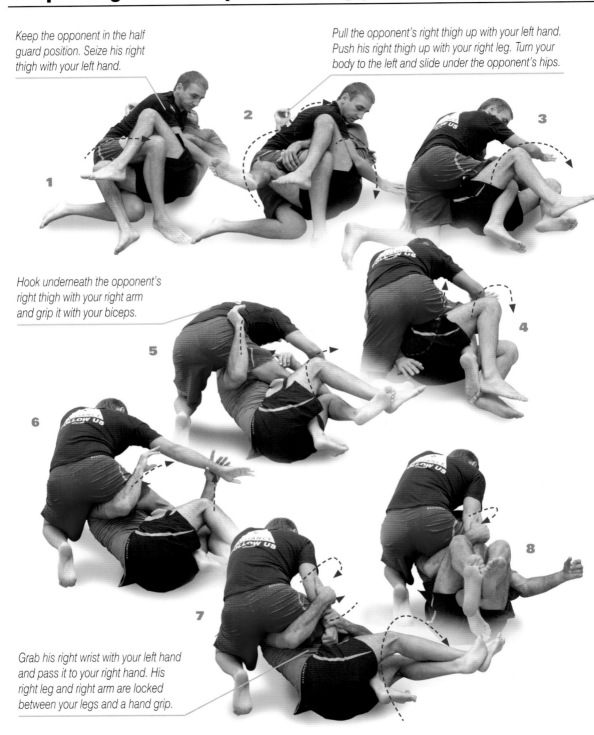

9

Rotate your body dynamically to the right. Roll with the opponent.

10

11

12

Continue to roll. Turn your opponent onto his back. Keep control over his right arm and right leg

13

14

The opponent is on his back. His right leg is locked. Slide your left arm underneath his neck. Assume the side control position.

Half guard sweep to mount

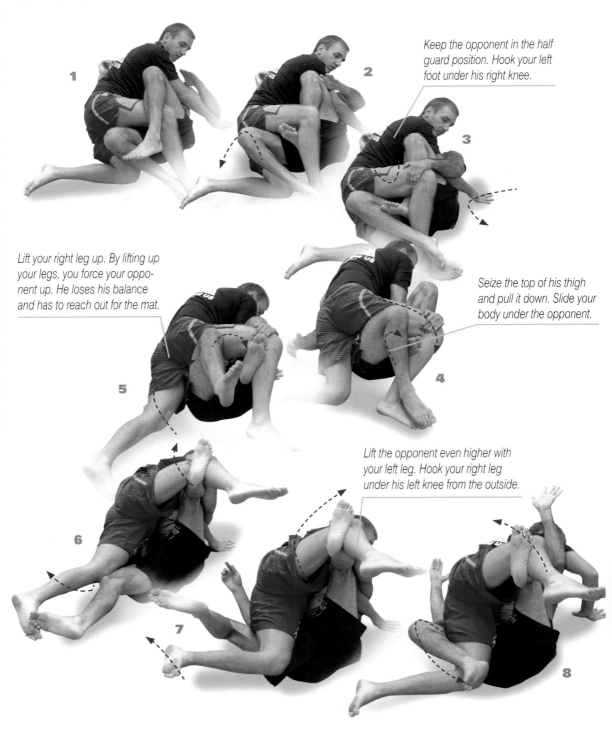

Keep the opponent in the half guard position. Hook your left foot under his right knee.

Lift your right leg up. By lifting up your legs, you force your opponent up. He loses his balance and has to reach out for the mat.

Seize the top of his thigh and pull it down. Slide your body under the opponent.

Lift the opponent even higher with your left leg. Hook your right leg under his left knee from the outside.

Force the opponent up with your left leg. Hook your right leg under his left leg from the outside. Your right hand pushes on his left thigh to help push him over.

Hook your right arm under the opponet's right arm and at the same time turn your body to the left. Force his left leg up. Roll with the opponent.

Hook your right arm under the opponent's right arm and at the same time turn your body to the left. Force his left leg up. Roll with the opponent.

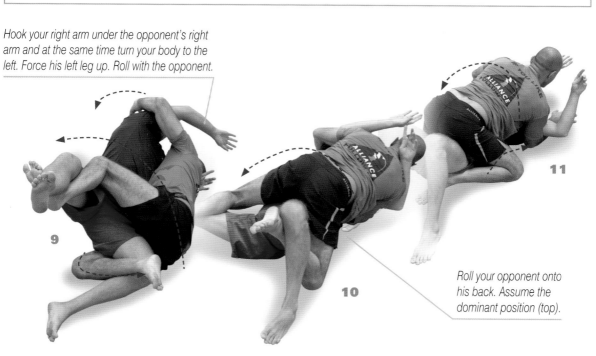

Roll your opponent onto his back. Assume the dominant position (top).

Half Guard without Gi   **173**

BRAZILIAN JIU-JITSU

Half guard sweep

Place your arms on the opponent's left shoulder and straighten your arms out. Shove him away from you. Your legs are hooked around his leg in a half guard.

You are on your right side. Seize the opponent's left leg with your left hand and pull it forward. Place your right hand under his left thigh.

At the same time, your right hand and your right leg force your opponent up and towards your head.

Hook his right knee with your right hand and his right calf with your left hand. Wrap your legs around the opponent's right thigh in the guard. Take his balance.

9

Push him backward. Grab his right arm to stop him from gaining his balance on the mat.

10

Roll your opponent onto his back. His right leg is locked between your thighs.

11

12

13

14

Keep the opponent in the half guard position. Hook your right arm underneath his left thigh. Wrap your left arm around his neck.

Half guard sweep dominating your opponent's legs

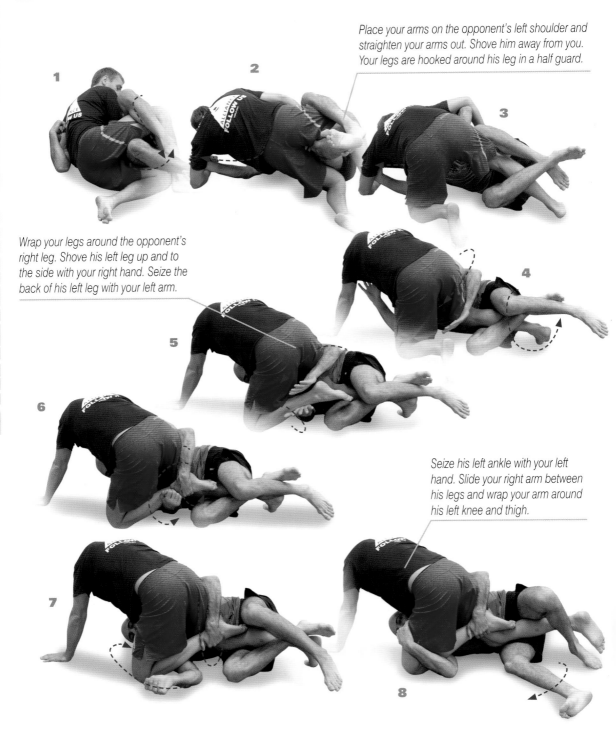

Place your arms on the opponent's left shoulder and straighten your arms out. Shove him away from you. Your legs are hooked around his leg in a half guard.

Wrap your legs around the opponent's right leg. Shove his left leg up and to the side with your right hand. Seize the back of his left leg with your left arm.

Seize his left ankle with your left hand. Slide your right arm between his legs and wrap your arm around his left knee and thigh.

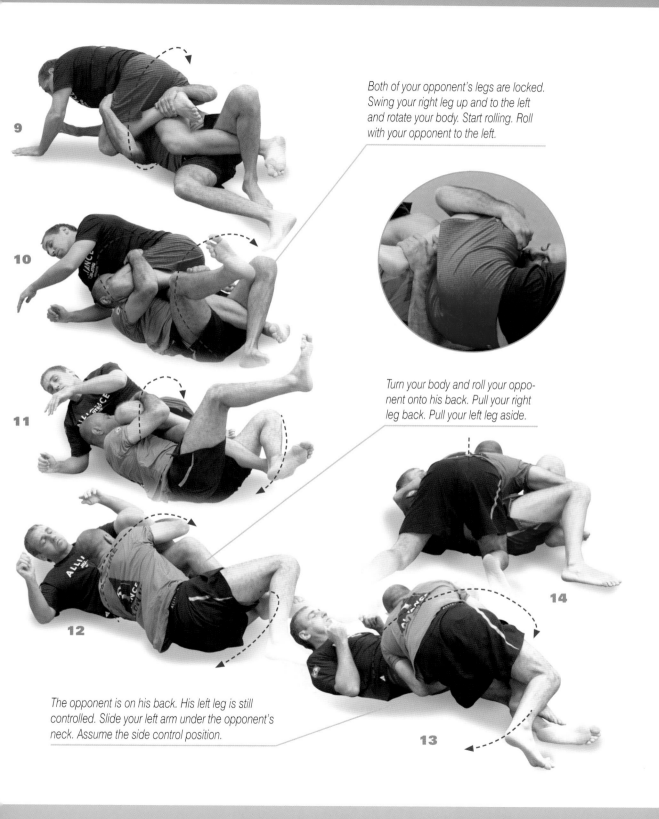

9

10

11

Both of your opponent's legs are locked. Swing your right leg up and to the left and rotate your body. Start rolling. Roll with your opponent to the left.

Turn your body and roll your opponent onto his back. Pull your right leg back. Pull your left leg aside.

14

12

13

The opponent is on his back. His left leg is still controlled. Slide your left arm under the opponent's neck. Assume the side control position.

Half guard sweep to side control

Place your arms on the opponent's left shoulder and straighten your arms out. Shove him away from you. Your legs are hooked around his leg in a half guard.

Wrap your legs around the opponent's right leg. Shove his left leg up and to the side with your right hand. Seize the back of his left leg with your left arm.

Both of your opponent's legs are locked. Swing your right leg up and to the left and rotate your body. Start rolling. Roll with your opponent to the left.

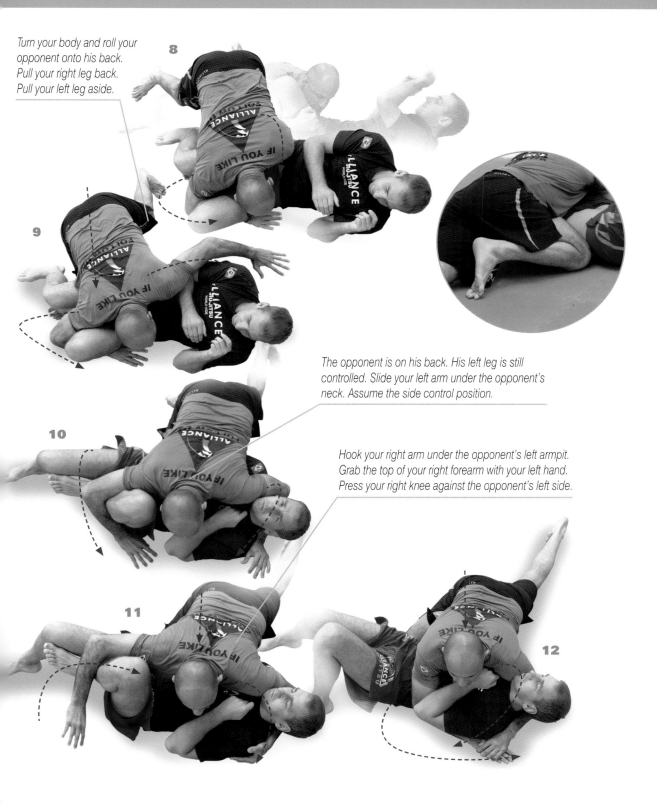

Turn your body and roll your opponent onto his back. Pull your right leg back. Pull your left leg aside.

The opponent is on his back. His left leg is still controlled. Slide your left arm under the opponent's neck. Assume the side control position.

Hook your right arm under the opponent's left armpit. Grab the top of your right forearm with your left hand. Press your right knee against the opponent's left side.

Deep half guard sweep to side control

Control the opponent in a half guard position. Seize his left thigh from the top with your left hand. Take the open position by pulling your left leg out from the guard.

Shift your body to the side. Slide your right arm under the opponent. Lift him up onto your right shoulder. The opponent loses his balance. He must steady himself on his hands.

Seize his right arm with your left hand and pass the grip to your right hand. His right arm is locked.

BRAZILIAN JIU-JITSU

Pull his right arm back with your right hand. Turn your body to the left. To strengthen the roll: seize the opponent's back with your left arm and pull.

Roll the opponent onto his back. Open the guard. Your right arm controls the opponent's right leg and hand.

Move your right leg over the opponent's right leg. Shove his hips aside with your knee. Your opponent is completely controlled.

Half guard pass to side control

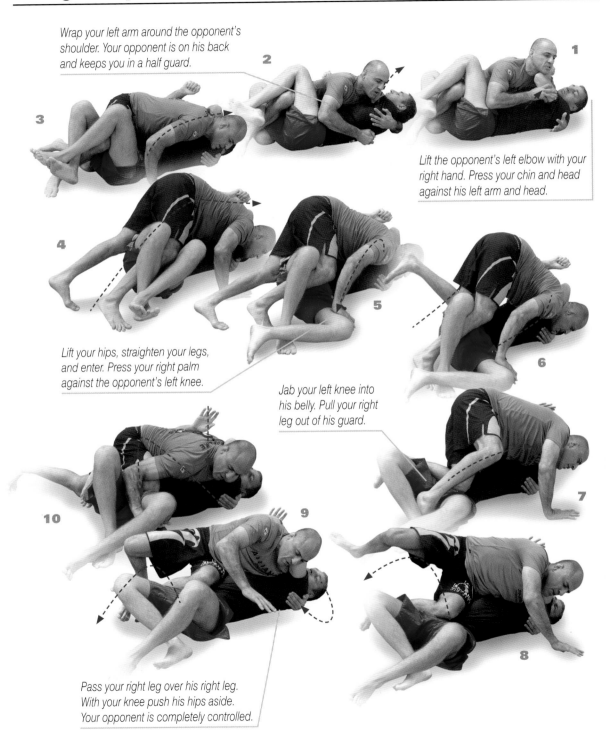

Wrap your left arm around the opponent's shoulder. Your opponent is on his back and keeps you in a half guard.

Lift the opponent's left elbow with your right hand. Press your chin and head against his left arm and head.

Lift your hips, straighten your legs, and enter. Press your right palm against the opponent's left knee.

Jab your left knee into his belly. Pull your right leg out of his guard.

Pass your right leg over his right leg. With your knee push his hips aside. Your opponent is completely controlled.

Half guard to Kimura pass

Hold the opponent's left shoulder with your left arm. Your opponent is on his back, keeping you in a half guard.

Control the opponent's left forearm with your right hand, so you can easily slide your left arm under his left armpit.

Grab the opponent's left wrist with your right hand. Your left hand grabs your right wrist – creating a keylock like in the kimura lock.

Stretch your body out. Extend your arms and legs. Free your right leg from the guard.

Your right leg is trapped in his guard. Keep a closed keylock (kimura).

BRAZILIAN JIU-JITSU

Half guard pass to knee cut across

Use your right thigh to shove his right thigh to the outside. Your opponent is shifted slightly to his side.

Slide your left hand under the opponent's neck. Shove his left leg down with your right hand.

Wrap your arms around the opponent and grip tightly. Thrust your body forward. Slide your knee onto his right hip.

Open your grip. Raise your hips and move your right knee over the opponent, to his right side

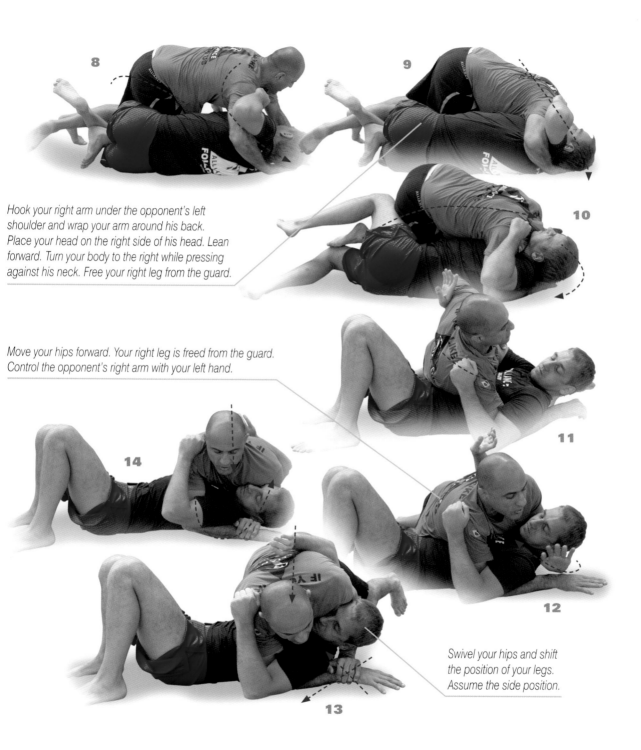

Hook your right arm under the opponent's left shoulder and wrap your arm around his back. Place your head on the right side of his head. Lean forward. Turn your body to the right while pressing against his neck. Free your right leg from the guard.

Move your hips forward. Your right leg is freed from the guard. Control the opponent's right arm with your left hand.

Swivel your hips and shift the position of your legs. Assume the side position.

CHAPTER 17

Attacking the Turtle Guard and Back Mount

Turtle guard attack to taking the back - arm bar finish

The turtle position. The opponent defends himself by kneeling and resting on his elbows.

Kneel on the opponent's left side. Grab the inside of his right forearm with both your hands. Hold the opponent tightly and roll forward, over his back.

Both your opponent's hands are locked in your grip. Tilt to the side and scoot your hips over. Lean back.

Hold the opponent's right arm from the top with your hands. Establish your position behind the opponent. Rest your feet on his hips.

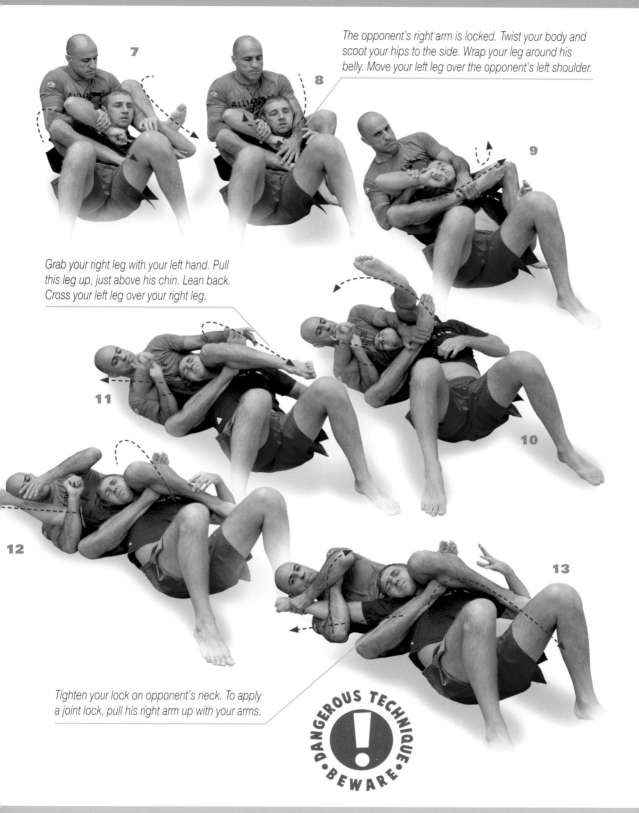

The opponent's right arm is locked. Twist your body and scoot your hips to the side. Wrap your leg around his belly. Move your left leg over the opponent's left shoulder.

Grab your right leg with your left hand. Pull this leg up, just above his chin. Lean back. Cross your left leg over your right leg.

Tighten your lock on opponent's neck. To apply a joint lock, pull his right arm up with your arms.

DANGEROUS TECHNIQUE
BEWARE
!

BRAZILIAN JIU-JITSU

Turtle guard attack to Kimura

The turtle position. The opponent defends himself by kneeling and resting on his elbows.

Kneel on the opponent's left side. Grab his right forearm from the inside with both your hands. Dynamically move around the opponent.

DANGEROUS TECHNIQUE • BEWARE •

Hold the opponent's right forearm from the inside with your right hand. Pull his right arm out. The opponent is forced to flip over.

Add your second hand to the grip. Apply the keylock to the opponent's forearm. Pull and twist the locked arm up.

Turtle guard attack to rear naked choke

The turtle position. The opponent defends himself by kneeling and resting on his elbows.

Kneel on the opponent's left side. Grab his right forearm from the inside with both your hands.

Hold your opponent tightly and lean back, taking him with you. Wrap your right leg over his hip, putting this leg on his right thigh.

Your left hand releases his forearm and wraps around his throat, then reaches out farther to grab his right biceps. Slide your right arm under his neck. Choke him.

DANGEROUS TECHNIQUE · BEWARE ·